GW00685014

ENTREPRENEURSHIP IN BRITAIN 1750–1939

Documents in Economic History

DOCUMENTS IN ECONOMIC HISTORY

General Editor: Professor Sidney Pollard, University of Sheffield

ENTREPRENEURSHIP IN BRITAIN 1750-1939

EDITED AND WITH AN INTRODUCTION BY

R. H. CAMPBELL
University of Stirling

and

R. G. WILSON
University of East Anglia

ADAM & CHARLES BLACK
LONDON

First published 1975
A. & C. Black Ltd., 4, 5 & 6 Soho Square, London W1V 6AD

© R. H. Campbell & R. G. Wilson, 1975
ISBN 0 7136 1524 9

All rights reserved. No part of this publication may be
reproduced, stored in a retrieval system, or transmitted, in
any form or by any means, electronic, mechanical, photo-
copying, recording or otherwise, without the prior permission in writing of A & C Black Ltd.

Designed by Richard Sadler Ltd.
Halfpenny Furze, Chalfont St. Giles,
Buckinghamshire.

Printed in Great Britain by
The Garden City Press Limited
Letchworth, Hertfordshire SG6 1JS

ACKNOWLEDGEMENTS

The editors and publishers wish to thank the following for permission to reproduce extracts taken from their works:

Harvard University Press for J. A. Schumpeter, *The Theory of Economic Development* (1934):
Professor W. G. Rimmer for a copy of John Marshall's manuscript 'Sketch of his Own Life':
The Business Archives Council for A. H. John (ed.), *The Walker Family Iron Founders and Lead Manufacturers 1741–1893* (1951):
The editor of *Business History* for R. G. Wilson, 'The Fortunes of a Leeds Merchant House, 1780–1820', *Business History*, IX (1967) and R. H. Campbell, 'The Financing of Carron Company', *Business History*, I (1958):
The Council of the Surtees Society for 'The Law Book of the Crowley Ironworks' (ed. M. W. Flinn), *Publications of the Surtees Society*, CLXVII (1957):
Penguin Books Ltd for their editions of Robert Owen, *A New View of Society* (1813) and *Report to the County of Lanark* (1820):
Mrs Mary Owens Crowther for H. Ford and S. Crowther, *My Life and Work* (1922):
Hutchinson Publishing Group Ltd for T. Lipton, *Leaves from the Lipton Logs* (1931):
James Clarke and Co. Ltd for their edition of John Calvin, *Institutes of the Christian Religion* (1953):
The John Rylands University Library of Manchester for letters from the Micklethwaite Papers (English Ms. 1138):
J. M. Dent and Sons Ltd for their Everyman editions of A. Smith, *The Wealth of Nations* and J. S. Mill, *On Liberty*:
Oxford University Press for their edition of S. Johnson, *Journey to the Western Isles of Scotland* (1961):
Eric Cregeen and the editor of the Association of Social Anthropologists Monographs, for 'The Changing Role of the House of Argyll in the Scottish Highlands' in I. M. Lewis (ed.), *History and Social Anthropology* (1968):
Weidenfeld (Publisher) Ltd for Nigel Nicolson, *Lord of the Isles* (1961).

Our thanks are due to Dr. T. R. Gourvish, Dr. J. M. Sanderson, Dr. M. I. Thomis and Dr. N. L. Tranter who have given us their good advice about this short volume of documents. We must also acknowledge the aid of our four typists, Miss P. Charman, Miss M. Hendry, Mrs. V. Striker and Mrs. B. Wilson who worked efficiently and cheerfully in Norwich and Stirling on our crabbed manuscript and endless photocopies.

CONTENTS

INTRODUCTION

I

Some historians give such prominence to the activities of individual businessmen or entrepreneurs that they write economic history as though it were the product of the actions of a few great men and the enterprise of a handful of key firms. The biographical approach has value, but, even if the excessively hagiographical approach of Samuel Smiles and other Victorian biographers is avoided, it fails to provide any satisfactory theory of the relationship between entrepreneurship and economic growth. For that an account of the life and work of any one man, no matter how great, cannot supply a tithe of the answers we should require.

Other historians encounter opposing difficulties by trying to provide an acceptable explanation of economic change through using the precise analytical methods of the natural sciences. Logical explanations of the rate and direction of economic development are imperilled by the hazards of accounting for the actions of human beings in a rational, consistent, and so predictable way. Human motivation may be rationalised through assuming the validity of certain economic objectives: that all maximise their profits and so will seek to lower costs and charge the most profitable price; or that labour will move to wherever wages are highest. The unreality of such assumptions, which lie behind the fiction of economic man, can easily be exposed in contemporary society, though less easily replaced by anything more acceptable. Lack of knowledge renders the problem even more acute in a historical context and is not always helped through the application of interpretations which may be applicable to the present time but not necessarily to the past. Hence attempts to place the contribution of the entrepreneur in the context of a general explanation of economic growth, past and present, are frequently confusing. The characteristics of the entrepreneur are as many as his interpreters; he may be thought rational and calculating, with a mind which was frequently a substitute for a computer before one had been invented; alternatively, he may be thought irrational and eccentric, yet shrewd for all that.

Moreover it is difficult to be judicious in commenting about business enterprises especially in the aggregate. Every historian has his own yardstick by which to evaluate performances. A firm can illustrate to one author every vice known to capitalism, to another the same firm will provide evidence of significant developments in management or accounting techniques. Both interpretations might have value, but because of this problem it is difficult to fit together a picture of a country's enterprise from individual case studies which are the life-blood of business history. And, therefore, the businessman can be given a major or a minor role, as preferred, and applauded or attacked by those who now survey his handiwork.

(i)

The need for an analysis of economic growth to allow for differences in knowledge or ability between societies has long been recognised. An early and conspicuous example is in the work of James Maitland, 8th Earl of Lauderdale, who criticised Adam Smith for his failure to make such allowances in the *Wealth of Nations*. Like most early economic writers before John Stuart Mill, Lauderdale did not distinguish capital and entrepreneurship and he was specifically concerned with providing an explanation of differences in the productivity of capital, and, as with Smith, saw the capitalist as a form of entrepreneur. In doing so he highlighted the contribution of the isolated acts of individuals in contributing to changes in the pattern of economic growth (Extract I). John Rae made the same point even more clearly and foreshadowed future interpretations by suggesting that invention was the key to the greater productivity of capital in some societies than in others (Extract II). Others, among them John Stuart Mill, recognised the need to take account of contrasts between societies in explanation of economic growth, but, in general, most theoretical discussion of the later nineteenth century tended to neglect the imponderables which the entrepreneur necessarily intruded into the increasingly mathematical explanations of economic phenomena.

Apart from the biographers, with their specialised contributions, many historians did likewise until increasing interest in the causes of industrialisation began to displace the interest in institutional studies. The causal contribution of the entrepreneur was soon recognised but as part of a general explanation, not as the central variable. So it was in such early, popular and well-established interpretations of the impulses to economic growth in Britain in the late eighteenth and early nineteenth centuries, as, first, the benefits of greater commercial and industrial freedom which followed the final crumbling of mercantilist restrictions, and second, (and even more popular) the benefits of the reductions in the costs of production which resulted from the introduction of new technology. In both explanations the entrepreneur's contribution was obscured through failure to distinguish his unique contribution from those of others; he played his part in the first as the propagandist in Manchester advocating free trade, and in the second as the inventor. Sometimes the connection was admitted only as an addition by way of an afterthought and, in any case, the connection was by no means always direct. The Manchester school's advocacy of free trade was vigorous only when the doctrine had been pioneered by others: by academics, by politicians, by civil servants: and there were other businessmen, especially in Birmingham, diametrically opposed to those in Manchester.

In any case commercial freedom was merely a necessary prerequisite of change. Hence the greater popularity of the interpretation which stressed the influence of the new technology. The spinning-jenny and the water-frame in cotton-spinning, the puddling process in iron manufacture; above all, the steam engine, so attracted the attention of those engaged in descriptive studies of industrialisation that they ousted many other possible explanations of the process from the field. If technical progress is placed at the centre of economic change, then the entrepreneur does not make the leading contribution for the role of inventors is not identical with the role of entrepreneurs during any period of industrialisation.

(ii)

Modern attempts to distinguish clearly the contribution of the entrepreneur, and at the same time to place his contribution at the centre of an explanation of economic growth, are best illustrated from the work of Joseph Schumpeter. Though in many ways he may be considered to have produced a brilliant exposition of ideas foreshadowed by Lauderdale, John Rae, even by J. S. Mill and others, Schumpeter's work can properly be regarded as a starting point of modern discussion and general assessment of the significance of entrepreneurial behaviour. He did not follow the earlier tradition which equated the contribution of capital and entrepreneurship but, following more in the tradition of J. B. Say, regarded entrepreneurship as a special, indeed a very special, form of labour. Schumpeter's exposition in the *Theory of Economic Development* is narrow and theoretical, though he demonstrated fully the historical significance of his work in subsequent studies.[1] His problem was to explain the breaks in the pattern of economic growth, or, more formally, how the tendency of the economy to move towards equilibrium was broken. His solution placed the role of the entrepreneur at the very centre of economic progress. It was the latter's unique ability to break out of the trend towards constant equilibrium in the economic system by devising new combinations of processes, products and markets. Innovation widely conceived in this way made the entrepreneur's contribution to development absolutely central in every branch of his multifarious activities, and therefore innovation and not invention became the basis of economic progress. By distinguishing innovation from invention Schumpeter led the discussion away from the tendency to identify the entrepreneur with the narrow contribution of the inventor or technologist and so provided a fuller and more personalised exposition of the various forces which earlier writers had recognised as determinants of differential rates

---

[1] For example in *Business Cycles* (1939), I, pp. 87–108. See also Schumpeter's, 'The creative Response in Economic History', *J. Econ. Hist.*, 7 (1949), pp. 149–59 and 'Economic Theory and Entrepreneurial History' in *Change and the Entrepreneur* (1949) also printed in H. G. J. Aiken *Explanations in Enterprise* (1965), pp. 45–64. The latter (pp. 3–25), and the first volume of *Explorations in Entrepreneurial History* (1949) provide discussions of Schumpeter's entrepreneurial theory.

of economic progress. Schumpeter thus provided the entrepreneur with a functional, not merely an institutional role that allowed him alone to initiate the discontinuities in economic expansion (Extract III).

(iii)

The relevance of Schumpeter's interpretation can be demonstrated in many phases of industrialisation, as in the following passages about three of the great 'Captains of Industry' of the classic Industrial Revolution—John Marshall, Sir Richard Arkwright and Josiah Wedgwood.[1] The first (Extract IV) taken from John Marshall's 'Sketch of his own life' is a rare personal declaration in which Marshall explicitly states that he wanted to break out of the confines of linen retailing which had provided an adequate living for his father. In its clear statement of objectives it illustrates perfectly Schumpeter's 'psychology of entrepreneurial activity'. The second (Extract V) taken from a Victorian biography of Samuel Crompton, brings out in its comparison of Crompton and Arkwright the fundamental differences in the qualities of the inventor and the innovator. Crompton was an inventor of genius who was temperamentally quite unable to create a successful firm to capitalise his important discovery: Arkwright on the other hand, the skilful adapter of other men's prototypes, drew a fat entrepreneurial profit from his ability to pioneer the factory production of roller-spun cotton yarns. The

[1] All three have been well served by recent economic historians: W. G. Rimmer's *Marshalls of Leeds, Flaxspinners*, 1788–1886 (1960) is a first-rate business history; for Arkwright see S. D. Chapman, *The Early Factory Masters* (1967) and R. S. Fitton and A. P. Wadsworth, *The Strutts and the Arkwrights* 1778–1830 (1958); Neil McKendrick has written extensively about Wedgwood: 'Josiah Wedgwood: An Eighteenth Century Entrepreneur in Salesmanship and Marketing Techniques', *Ec. H.R.*, xii (1960), pp. 408–33; 'Josiah Wedgwood and Factory Discipline', *The Historical Journal*, IV (1961), pp. 30–55; 'Josiah Wedgwood and Thomas Bentley: An Inventor-Entrepreneurship Partnership in the Industrial Revolution', *Trans. R. Hist. Soc.*, 14 (1964), pp. 1–33; Josiah Wedgwood and Cost Accounting in the Industrial Revolution', *Ec. H.R.*, XXIII (1970), pp. 45–67. See also his recent critical review of various Victorian histories of the Potteries (including Meteyard), 'The Victorian View of Midland History: A Historiographical Study of the Potteries', *Midland History*, I (1972), pp. 34–47.

third (Extract VI), from a Victorian life of Josiah Wedgwood, shows that the gap between nineteenth-century industrial biography and Schumpeter is in some senses not wide. The language is different of course: where Schumpeter linked psychology and entrepreneurship in fairly abstract theory, Samuel Smiles, and here Miss Meteyard, underlined the moral uprightness, the successful struggle against adversity of their subjects. Nevertheless underlying both there is the same emphasis on hard work, vision and constant experiment and innovation that were the hallmarks of the successful entrepreneurs and which set them apart in their contribution to the expansion of their own particular industries.

II

An analysis of the entrepreneurial function in general must be supplemented by an examination of the particular qualities which lead some entrepreneurs to greater success than others. Different commentators isolate and stress different contributions as the essence of the entrepreneur's role: notably as a financier; as an organiser of production; and as a salesman.

(i)

The financial activities of the entrepreneur have been placed at the heart of many explanations of economic growth because many emphasise the need to ensure an adequate and ready supply of capital. Adam Smith stressed the contribution of capital accumulation in increasing the wealth of nations, and more modern emphasis on the causal role of capital investment, first in theories of economic fluctuations, and then in theories of economic growth, led historians to such preoccupation with this issue, that 'there is a greater danger that the importance of capital in relation to economic progress will be exaggerated than that it will be underrated'.[1]

It is easy to overstate the significance of capital investment to the economic progress of Britain in the eighteenth century simply

---

[1] A. K. Cairncross, *Factors in Economic Development* (1962), p. 88.

because there was a marked growth of financial institutions and practices in the period. Yet since the escalation of the national debt was one of the most striking features of the eighteenth century the expansion rested more on government than on private industrial borrowing. But capital which might have found its way into industrial use was not drained away into largely unproductive government investment because there is little evidence which suggests that industry was starved of capital. The leading sectors in the industrial revolution, particularly the textile industries, had relatively little need of it. Between 1780 and 1800 investment in the cotton and iron industries was only about ten per cent in value of the national debt at the outbreak of the French Wars in 1793. Business grew by the assiduous plough-back of profits and the application of important but frequently low cost advances in technology.[1] A famous example of the emergence of a leading firm working on these principles and starting from the smallest origins is provided by the Walkers of Rotherham (Extract VII).

Though it is important not to exaggerate the need for financial capital in the aggregate, need was sometimes vitally important for the success of an individual enterprise, or in a particular area or at a critical time. At such junctures the provision of adequate financial aid could make the difference between the success or failure of an enterprise. Extract VIII shows the strains imposed on a firm which was expanding its output quickly by extensive mechanisation and at the same time launching its products into the export trade. The operation was doubly difficult because it was attempted during a period of war and the market—Latin America—was entirely new. Aid from the firm's bankers made the whole venture possible and a pushing industrialist was thereby allowed the fullest opportunities. Yet it was not the essential function of the entrepreneur to provide funds personally; frequently he borrowed, helped to do so by an increasingly efficient capital market and by a low rate of interest. Provided the entrepreneur had other qualities to offer, the capital came from

---

[1] See F. Crouzet (ed.), *Capital Formation in the Industrial Revolution* (1972), especially Crouzet's introduction and the key articles of Heaton and Pollard, reprinted there; also S. D. Chapman, 'Fixed Capital Formation in the British Cotton Industry 1770–1815, *Ec. H.R.*, xxiii (1970), pp. 235–66.

other sources, as from the land, when rents rose through the pressure of the demand of a rising population for food, and from successful merchants and traders. Sometimes a landlord, or, more commonly a trader became an industrialist. Then there was no need to borrow. But the lack of the personal possession of funds did not hold back the successful entrepreneur. If he had the necessary qualities for survival, he could obtain the funds. Ownership of adequate resources was a far less important ingredient of success than shrewd financial management.

Carron Company founded in 1759, was an unusually large enterprise for its day and required such substantial capital inputs that resources were severely strained and a new manager, Charles Gascoigne, had to mount a major rescue operation, which required the exercise of financial ability of a high quality.[1] His efforts demonstrate the extent to which capital could be obtained from a multitude of sources, yet how in itself even such ready access to the supply of capital did not ensure the success of the company. For that, other entrepreneurial qualities were necessary (Extract IX).

(ii)

If the ability to supply adequate financial capital is regarded as a useful adjunct but not as an essential ingredient in entrepreneurial success, ability to organise the process of production may be of the essence. Some regard such ability as so critical to the success of business enterprise that they distinguish it as a factor of production separate from the traditional trinity of land, labour and capital (Extracts X 1 and 2).

Some of the most conspicuous problems in industrialisation emerge in the organisation of production, because, following Schumpeter once again, the new combinations are often to be found in the new processes of production: new industrial locations; new operations; a new labour force to be adapted and trained for the new techniques. The vastness of such social and economic changes within the individual firm can easily be ignored

---

[1] For a full account of Carron Company see R. H. Campbell, *Carron Company* (1961).

in an aggregative or statistical analysis. Being able to deal with them was a managerial problem, though not one delegated to a paid employed managerial class until the later nineteenth century. By then the problem was much easier to tackle in Britain, as so many of the aspects of industrial discipline, fiercely resisted earlier, had become common form in an industrial society. The successful entrepreneur was he who could solve such entirely new industrial problems. Doing so seems to have required a combination of an ability to attend to detail and to take authoritarian action wherever necessary; qualities which may be illustrated from the work of two successful entrepreneurs, separated by over half a century: Ambrose Crowley and Robert Owen. Both are useful examples for they are frequently remembered for their philanthropic rather than their entrepreneurial quality. Ambrose Crowley, who died in 1713, had a large ironworks in County Durham and ran it from London through a system codified in a Law Book. Historians have used the Law Book for examples of industrial paternalism: aid to the sick and aged; funeral benefits; provision of schools, doctors and ministers. But the Law Book also demonstrates marked commercial acumen, of which the social paternalism was a by-product. Like a modern textbook on scientific management, it lays out an established chain of command through an elaborate system of committees, devised to provide a system of checks and balances which would eliminate dishonesty and neglect. Crowley may have been a paternalist employer; he was also an exacting one, whose schemes were aimed at ensuring maximum efficiency by authoritarian attention to the details of production (Extract XI).[1]

Robert Owen too is probably best remembered for his pioneering co-operative and educational measures, but, once again, much of his concern may be attributed to that authoritarian paternalism which enabled him to succeed in paying attention to the range of detail required in primitive industrial concerns. Certainly Owen applied techniques to the organisation of his labour force which to the modern mind do not marry easily with some of his social

---

[1] Professor M. W. Flinn has in addition to editing the Law Book written the history of the Crowleys in *Men of Iron, The Crowleys in the Early Iron Industry* (1962).

2—EIB * *

philosophy, as in his attempts to encourage maximum production through the display of a system of coloured discs above each worker, the colours showing to the world the merits of a particular worker. Owen built his success on the career of his father-in-law, David Dale. His account of Dale's activities, and of his own problems at New Lanark, illustrate the detail to which the entrepreneur had to attend and the social concern was frequently the outcome of the attempt to promote economic objectives (Extract XII).[1]

(iii)

The need for an authoritarian regime, or for a deliberate policy of conciliation, reflected the need to assuage the opposition engendered by the 'new methods of production', but no matter how efficiently they were organised, ability to sell the product was also required. Technical change, even by cutting costs, will not lead to economic success unless it is accompanied by ability to sell. If the market analysis is correct, and an appropriate sales policy followed in the first instance, success may be possible even with high costs of production. Several well-known examples for Britain during the industrial revolution can be cited: James Watt's patent for the steam engine became a commercial success only when Matthew Boulton, with his ability to market the device on suitable terms, assumed the share of the patent previously held by the scientifically acute but commercially incompetent, John Roebuck;[2] Josiah Wedgwood, the potter, succeeded more through his knowledge of how to exploit a snob market than through his technical ability which could be copied.[3] A century later the principle remained, but the practice changed through the rise of a mass market, as many in more affluent societies rose above a subsistence standard of living and so could afford to acquire luxuries for the first time ever. Henry Ford saw the possibilities of

---

[1] Three recent books have dealt very fully with various aspects of Owen's career and influence: J. Butt (ed.) *Robert Owen, Prince of Cotton Spinners* (1971); J. F. C. Harrison, *Robert Owen and the Owenites in Britain and America* (1969); S. Pollard and J. Salt (eds.) *Robert Owen Prophet of the Poor* (1971).

[2] J. Lord, *Capital and Steam Power 1750–1800* (1923), pp. 90–130.

[3] See note, p. 13

such a market and organised the production of his cars accordingly; most British manufacturers did not do so[1] (Extract XIII).

All was not lost in Britain at that time for a new pushing generation of retailers did see the prospects of smaller, but nevertheless growing, mass market at home and through changing their pattern of sales produced perhaps the greatest entrepreneurs in Britain of the late nineteenth century. They were the counterparts to the better known entrepreneurs (the Boultons, the Wedgwoods, the Owens) of a century earlier. A notable aspect of their market sense was the exploitation of advertising. Extract XIV provides a striking illustration in this field in the work of Thomas Lipton.[2]

III

Whatever weight may be given to the entrepreneurial qualities already examined, or whatever others may be added, human nature is sufficiently variable to ensure the irregular advent of Schumpeter's new economic combinations and so the discontinuity of economic growth. On the other hand, the extent of their possession and exploitation is not the result of individual merit and demerit, perhaps even the by-products of chance genetic factors, for the entrepreneur works in a historical situation and the social environment may be favourable or hostile to his activities. An excellent survey of the influences which operate on the entrepreneur's environment and the constraints they place upon his actions was given by J. S. Mill (Extract XV). An extreme interpretation places such stress on the contribution of a particular environment that economic growth comes to be explained in terms which are virtually those of physical determinism, as when the contribution of natural endowments is given such prominence that little room is left for individual human initiative. This view is

---

[1] S. B. Saul, 'The Motor Industry in Britain to 1914', *Business History*, V (1963), pp. 22–44.
[2] See C. Wilson, 'Economy and Society in Late Victorian Britain', *Ec. H.R.*, XVIII (1965), pp. 183–98; J. B. Jefferys, *Retail Trading in Britain 1850–1950* (1965); P. Mathias, *Retailing Revolution* (1967) for discussion about the profound changes in retailing after 1870.

no longer advanced in the crude form which was once current, but it still lingers. The relevance of a whole string of natural factors—coal, climate, communications—may be admitted as determinants of economic change. Inadequate or expensive coal supplies in France may be advanced as a major factor retarding its growth; and the industrial growth of the north of England was dependent on the peculiar importance of coal as a source of power in the nineteenth century. The answer to the extreme physical determinist is simple. Favourable natural endowments facilitate economic growth, but their exploitation rests on a variety of influences. In France the retardation of economic growth in the nineteenth century was not merely a reflection of natural factors: it may have rested as much on the inadequacies of the country's entrepreneurs.[1] Comparison with the contribution of technology in economic growth is apposite.

Alone, liberal natural endowments, or a high level of technological achievement, must await exploitation or application before they have economic effects. The determinism of the physical scientists has never had an influence comparable to that of social scientists, but in their attempts to provide a more satisfactory alternative sociologists and economists have encountered the ever-present danger of trying to compress historical experience into a model almost as mechanistic and determinist as the explanations

---

[1] One of the best debates about entrepreneurship and economic development centres on the example of nineteenth-century France. See D. Landes, 'French Entrepreneurship and Industrial Growth in the Nineteenth Century', *J. Econ. Hist.* (1949), pp. 45–61; 'French Business and the Businessmen in Social and Cultural Analysis' in E. M. Earle (ed.), *Modern France* (1951), pp. 334–54; J. E. Sawyer, 'Strains in the social structure of Modern France', in Earle, pp. 293–312; 'The Entrepreneur and the Social Order, France and the United States' in W. Miller, *Men in Business* (1952), pp. 7–22. Landes' and Sawyer's assertions about the importance of social attitudes in explaining retardation in nineteenth-century France have been fiercely challenged by A. Gerschenkron, 'Social Attitudes, Entrepreneurship and Economic Development', *Ex. Ent. Hist.*, 6 (1953–4), pp. 1–19, 287–93, 297. Landes and Sawyer both made replies in the volume of this same journal, pp. 245–86. A convenient summary of the above, with some constructive comparison from the British case, is to be found in C. P Kindleberger, *Economic Growth in France and Britain 1851–1950* (1964), 113–34. Landes has continued using sociological theories in his study of European economic development, see *The Unbound Prometheus* (1969), but his use of these methods was given a very hostile review by Rondo Cameron in *Ex. Ent. Hist.*, 8 (1970–1), pp. 229–37.

of the physical scientists. The accusation is not primarily against the lack of realism of some of the theoretical explanations of social and economic change, but, more fundamentally, against the assumption that any consistent, or worse still, any inevitable patterns can be devised. Marx and from a totally different standpoint Rostow's stages theory have been challenged on these grounds. Both provide insight into the process of change, but—even allowing for Rostow's assumption that the appearance of a business élite is one of the pre-conditions for economic growth—they are in danger of making inadequate provision for the human initiative of the entrepreneur being able to encourage or distort economic development. Recent work on why rates of economic growth should differ between countries and over time has led to a fuller recognition of the range of variables to be taken into account in any full explanation, and in particular to the improbability of increasing economic growth simply by augmenting the supplies of factors of production.[1] So the contribution of the entrepreneur, though not necessarily its exact form, has come to be recognised as more central than ever to the process of development. The range of new economic combinations is immense and the choice of one rather than another is in the last analysis an exercise in human, or entrepreneurial, judgment. Since the exercise of such choice is conditioned by the environment, much attention has been given to investigating ways in which a particular environment is more likely to produce a race of capable businessmen than another. Many suggestions have come, from all the social sciences, advancing the claims of one or other influence.

(i)

One factor, popular, yet with a respectable ancestry bred out of Weber and Tawney, is the influence of religious belief in forming successful entrepreneurs.[2] The interpretation cannot go far and

---

[1] E. F. Denison, *Why Growth Rates Differ* (1967); R. C. O. Mathews, 'Some Aspects of Post-War Growth in the British Economy in Relation to Historical Experience', *Transactions of the Manchester Statistical Society* (1964–5), pp. 1–25; W. E. G. Salter, *Productivity and Technical Change* (1960).

[2] M. Weber, *The Protestant Ethic and the Spirit of Capitalism* (1930); R. H. Tawney, *Religion and the Rise of Capitalism* (1922).

still retain agreement among its supporters. Variations are legion: the causal factor may be protestantism, or puritanism, or dissent. The varieties of interpretation alone make the view suspect. More important, the supposed connection between a particular theological standpoint and entrepreneurial success has never been demonstrated. Perhaps the fault lies with historians. Ecclesiastical historians may have been too concerned with the niceties of disputes over church order and have paid insufficient attention to the influence of changing doctrine on economic man. Economic and social historians have then been forced to find their own theological evidence to explain economic success. Of course, any strongly held intellectual position must influence character and the ability to tackle problems of any kind, be they economic or otherwise. Most would therefore accept that any firm religious conviction will be a major determinant of the qualities which make for entrepreneurial success. The exact form of the influence is a matter of dispute, for it is extremely difficult to prove that any particular theological position is sufficiently precise to form the character requisite to initiate economic change and to carry it out. Further, the position of an individual theologian may be clear, but not necessarily the practical deductions for economic policy which follow from his position. Calvin is an example, for he can identify either riches or poverty as representing the will of God (Extract XVI). Other theologians can lead to an even more awkward dilemma. Even though the process of accumulating riches may be considered the inevitable outcome of a Christian life, their accumulation can give rise to snares in the path of Christian living (Extract XVII).

The difficulties of providing any clear and positive link between a particular theological position and the qualities which make for a successful entrepreneur lead some to hold that the contribution of theologians was mainly the negative but fundamental Protestant doctrine of freeing the individual from any form of external restraints, for theological restraints which led to any contrived acceptance of the traditional social fabric inhibited moves towards any form of change, economic or otherwise. In such a way the Protestant contribution could be positive, by breaking down social conventions and inhibitions between the religious and the secular, so that God could be glorified by actions previously categorised as religious. If the secular was thus made religious, a positive theological encouragement was given to economic action. The entrepreneur was as worthy an occupation as that of the theologian. Any similar spiritual encouragement is equally potent and examples may be provided from different systems of thought. A poem by George Herbert illustrates the sublimation of the secular in this way in a striking form (Extract XVIII).

The stress on religious belief is on safer ground when it is seen to operate only indirectly, and perhaps even incidentally through other factors which have a more evident economic influence. For example, Dissenters may have been more successful entrepreneurs in England in the eighteenth century, not directly because of the tenets of their religious faith, but, indirectly, because their faith excluded them from much official life, with all its opportunities and distractions, and because they were better educated.[1] Moreover their worship was organised in a very different way from the Church of England. They themselves paid their minister. It was an important difference that gave a caucus of the more well-to-do members of any chapel real authority and commitment and a knowledge of the spiritual and material well-being of each other in a way that was unknown in the Anglican Church. Thus the structure of Dissenting worship, rather than any peculiar tenets of faith, gave rise to those remarkable business partnerships which dominated so many key firms in the eighteenth and nineteenth centuries.

(ii)

The general principle may be acceptable but, as with religion, it is difficult to determine the exact form by which a particular education fitted a businessman for his function, and once again the influence may be general, though still potent. In Britain in the

---

[1] There is no good single account of eighteenth-century Dissent. Irene Parker, *Dissenting Academies in England* (1914) provides an early and readable discussion of its role in education. T. S. Ashton, himself a Dissenter, stressed in many of his writings the numerous ways in which Dissent and industry were linked; but these views have been questioned in N. Hans, *New Trends in Education in the Eighteenth Century* (1951) and K. Samuelson, *Religion and Economic Action* (1961).

late eighteenth and early nineteenth centuries education in accordance with a specific pattern of curriculum was less necessary than education to accept and to initiate rational changes in any walk of life, in this case in economic activities.[1] A willingness to devise and apply new ideas, to receive them from and pass them to others, an education which enabled the recipient to grasp the relevance of his studies and so inculcate general application, was more necessary than the subjection to a particular curriculum. The approach of the Scottish universities may have been more helpful to nascent entrepreneurs than the content of the instruction they received in them for these reasons, and the difference between the Scottish and English universities, as outlined by Adam Smith makes the point forcefully (Extract XIX).

The connection between education and the entrepreneur is easier to understand in Britain in the later nineteenth century for it is then more demonstrable. Successful industrial development then relied on greater technical expertise than during the earlier stages of industrialisation. Advances in science and industry became more clearly linked. In the past important, but simple technical discoveries had been largely based upon the empirical experimentation of a few forward thinking businessmen. Now as developments in iron and steel, chemicals and the uses of electricity outpaced progress in the textile industries scientific education assumed a new significance in the businessman's make-up. As with so many other qualities, however, the entrepreneur did not need to possess such ability himself, provided that he was willing to encourage others to acquire the knowledge and then to give them the maximum opportunity to apply it. There is some

---

[1] The role of the entrepreneur in providing education is considered in Michael Sanderson 'Education and the Factory in Industrial Lancashire, 1780–1840', *Ec. H.R.*, XX (1967), pp. 266–79; L. Wynne Evans, *Education in Industrial Wales 1700–1900, a study of the Works School System* (1971). The relationship of the Victorian businessman to the public schools has been unravelled in T. W. Bamford, *The Rise of the Public Schools* (1967), chapter 5, p. 9; T. J. H. Bishop and R. Wilkinson, *Winchester and the Public School Elite* (1967) and D. Ward, 'The Public Schools and Industry in Britain after 1870', *Journal of Contemporary History*, 2 (1967). The early shortcomings of the universities as providers of a businessman's education (and recipients of his patronage) are considered in E. Ashby, *Technology and the Academics* (1958) and Michael Sanderson, *The Universities and British Industry 1850–1970* (1972).

evidence to support the view that the British businessman of the late nineteenth century was reluctant to take this course. Blame for this unfortunate state of affairs cannot easily be attributed.

Several criticisms were advanced by contemporaries at all levels of the British educational system: lack of properly trained staff, funds and facilities; scarcity and incompetence of science teachers in schools, the conservatism of the universities themselves; and the indifference of the public. Comparisons, particularly with the German educational system, revealed inadequacies that became more alarming as our competitive position overseas was increasingly threatened by Germany and America. Yet almost every ambitious businessman was eager to consign his sons to learn classics and acquire varying degrees of polish at some English public school, schools which of course proliferated at this period because of his predilection. Here the criticism centres more upon the English social system than upon the deficiencies of the educational system in itself but the economic costs were obvious. If British businessmen were less effective than their German and American rivals in the late nineteenth century the educational background of many second and third generation entrepreneurs goes some way towards providing an explanation. As the fate of the Glasgow School of Mines indicates (Extracts XX and XXI) the entrepreneur in that area, in which the heavy industries were beginning to feel the chill winds of foreign competition, failed to appreciate the contribution which scientific and technical instruction may have made to the maintenance of their competitive position. One example may seem inadequate, but the deficiencies of the entrepreneurs in this field were more general (Extract XXII).

In the early stages of industrialisation in Britain the provision of some form of education for the mass of the labour force was perhaps even more necessary for economic success than the access to the highest level of contemporary technical knowledge. The educational provision required by an economy is not always identical at all times and places. Just as technical knowledge may have been less necessary in the early part of the nineteenth century than it was later, so it was with the need to provide a generally educated labour force. But, whatever the specific educational needs, the responsibility of providing it in Britain fell on the entrepreneur until the later nineteenth century. Robert Owen was a conspicuous example of an entrepreneur who did so, but as part of a general educational or social philosophy (Extract XXIII). Others did so less theoretically (Extract XXIV) and in other cases entrepreneurial and ecclesiastical action combined (Extract XXV). In few cases was education designed in any precise way to produce economic benefits. Not all were motivated in the ways of Robert Owen, but there is little evidence that the uphill task many of them undertook was for deliberate economic gain. Even when the more enlightened provided educational services, the entrepreneurs of the industrial revolution in Britain hardly appreciated its economic significance.

Direct links between education or religion and entrepreneurial success are equally difficult to decipher. Their influences may be more general by encouraging those changes in social structure and opinion which facilitate the formation of new economic combinations by the successful entrepreneurs. Hence the two influences can be linked intimately. The foundation of the English dissenting academies and the reformation of the Scottish universities, was influenced by religious belief, even though as a by-product. In such cases a religious situation produced an education system suitable for the encouragement of commercial initiative. Similarly the nationalist sentiment and the social conditions of Germany in the nineteenth century may have provided an educational system equally conducive to successful entrepreneurial initiative. In one case the motivation may have been religious and in the other the outcome of some form of nationalist sentiment, but both may be the product of some more fundamental, common forces. If so the historian must search for an explanation of how some individuals are more able than others to exploit the favourable opportunities opened up by an operation of educational and religious and other forces making for change in the environment. And that is still the key issue: the question of how the qualities which make for entrepreneurial success are implanted in the individual.

(iii)

To the solution of the problem psychologists have advanced a number of useful suggestions: especially through their stress on the wide range of human needs which determine the motivation of the individual: above all, perhaps, the need for achievement.[1] How such motives are implanted in the individual in the first place is much less easy to determine, especially when, for example, it is a question of how a particular form of motivation, which encouraged commercial enterprise, could be so effectively implanted in many individuals at a time such as the British industrial revolution. A possible explanation, which has been advanced, and which coalesces with the older stress on dissent, is that the dissenters had the appropriate motivation for industrial success because of the way they were brought up. The method of rearing children (and so the implanting in them of the motives conducive to certain economic activities, such as the need for achievement) may then explain why some groups of people produced more businessmen than others. Extract XXVI shows the pressure of these practices on a youth from an early nineteenth-century business family. This rare survival of a schoolboy's correspondence in which the father stresses the necessity to succeed, illustrates a theme which was by no means uncommon among the middle classes.

But the above argument still has a major gap. While it explains how society may help to produce and condition the entrepreneur, it does not explain why only some businessmen succeed. Success cannot be correlated simply with the character of the individual for that would lead to social and economic change resting entirely on the heroic actions of the individual businessman. So, just as one society rather than another may help the growth of those qualities in the individual which lead to the success of the entrepreneur, so one society rather than another may provide external conditions which make the task of the entrepreneur easier than others. Some forms of social action make an easily recognised contribution to the success of the individual, as, for example, the causal contribution to the British industrial revolution of the new found commercial freedom which followed the

---

[1] D. C. McLelland, *The Achieving Society* (1961). See also E. E. Hagen, *On the Theory of Social Change* (1964) and T. Burns and S. B. Saul (eds.) *Social Theory and Economic Change* (1967), pp. 9–34, where M. W. Flinn gives a good, succinct review of the difficulties of relating recent social theories to explanations of our industrialisation.

removal of mercantilist restrictions. Other social influences have more directly encouraged the actions of the entrepreneur. As might be expected, businessmen had been more successful in societies which did not regard industry and commerce as occupations which should be confined only to some of its members, whether of high or low status. Otherwise the supply of commercial talent was restricted.

A similar situation may have existed in England in the late nineteenth century.[1] 'Merchants are commonly ambitious of becoming country gentlemen'—Adam Smith's view of the late eighteenth century was even more applicable by the late nineteenth century.[2] Industry may always be something to get out of, to provide an opportunity to indulge the flesh or the mind according to choice. But, if there is social pressure to leave business, or not to go into it at all, the supply of talent is affected. Moreover the size of firms in some industries now precluded almost all but the existing owners of capital so that leadership was often confined to men of fixed outlooks about opportunities. Restriction of entry usually meant conservatism. Nineteenth-century England therefore illustrates the economic changes of social demarcation. The problem was partly education. Education for a cultural élite, characteristic of England, produced an educational system which served the country much less well in a modern economy. The problem was also cultural for some of those reared in such an educational system felt unable to take non-professional employment even when it might have been in their interest to do so (Extract XXVII).

Such social determinants are as much part of the environment in which the individual operates as the more commonly required physical determinants. Both may limit, or extend, the freedom of

---

[1] The debate about the role of the entrepreneur in Britain's economic slowdown after 1870 has been one of the more stimulating and inconclusive controversies of recent years. See D. H. Aldcroft, 'The Entrepreneur and the British Economy, 1870–1914', *Ec. H.R.*, XVII (1964), pp. 113–34; A. L. Levine, *Industrial Retardation in Britain, 1880–1914* (1967); S. B. Saul, *The Myth of the Great Depression* (1969); D. N. McCloskey and L. G. Sandberg, 'From Damnation to Redemption: Judgments on the Late Victorian Entrepreneur', *Explorations in Economic History*, 9 (1971), No. 1, pp. 89–108; D. C. Coleman, 'Gentlemen and Players', *Ec. H.R.*, XXVI (1972), pp. 92–116.

[2] A. Smith, *Wealth of Nations* (Cannan edition), I, p. 382.

action to the individual, and so render him less or more a free agent. To varying degrees the individual entrepreneur is therefore the creature rather than the creator of his environment.

The relevance of such social constraints has been recognised in the social philosophies of writers of different standpoints. Adam Smith accepted the need for civil government as a means of protecting property, which was necessary in more advanced societies (Extract XXVIII). Engels and Marx recognised that the success of the bourgeoisie arose when their forceful qualities encouraged the development of capitalist institutions favourable to their activities (Extract XXIX). J. S. Mill, held that individuality was the main force making for progressive change. While recognising that in his day business was the only field where it still operated, he pointed out the ultimate dangers which would follow from failure to encourage individuality to the full (Extract XXX).

Smith, Marx and Mill provide very different examples of how different societies may encourage, or indeed make possible, some form of economic enterprise. So in modern times the growth of such new institutional developments as professional management, joint-stock companies and state intervention have also influenced the form of action required of the successful entrepreneur. Though such changes in the environment in which the entrepreneur works, be they philosophical or institutional, change the form and extent of actions required, they do not affect the essential qualities of entrepreneurial behaviour. The qualities requisite for economic success are more constant, though their effectiveness may vary because of environmental changes. The significance of such external influences is highlighted by the way in which a region, even when part of a country generally industrialised, may still reject the assumptions on which industrial society, and so the motivation of the businessman, is based. Such conditions operated in the Scottish Highlands.

Dr Johnson distinguished the unusual function of the tacksman, but his identification of him with Crowley, the ironmaster, assumed erroneously that they were similarly motivated. The tacksman's objectives were social or military, not economic, hence they failed to provide entrepreneurial stimulus they might otherwise have given to the Highland economy. The fault may have been in the deficiencies in the personal qualities of the tacksman, but his task was difficult in the Highlands where many assumed an inalienable right to the land and were reluctant to encourage innovations which led to change in the conventional social order (Extract XXXI).[1] Dr Cregeen shows by combining the techniques of the historian with ideas borrowed from the social anthropologists, how this traditional society 'was dragged into the modern world by the coercion of the house of Argyll' (Extract XXXII). Here entrepreneurial vision rested entirely with the Dukes and some of their more forward looking agents in their enormous task of attempting to force the Highlander to conform to the values of the more advanced industrial society of the Lowlands. The work of Lord Leverhulme in the Highlands fifty years ago illustrates perfectly the magnitude of the problems an entrepreneur had to face in an environment where different social assumptions were at work. Half a century's experience in business, a tremendous reputation as a superbly successful entrepreneur were of little use in this situation. Even though the historian of his work there believes that his idea would have been basically sound on the reasonable assumption that the European market for fish were to be as secure after 1918 as before 1914, he also demonstrates the way in which even such a great entrepreneur could fail in a strange environment (Extract XXXIII). If Lord Leverhulme was defeated in a society still not ready for his plans, much more so less capable entrepreneurs. So the entrepreneur is not necessarily a heroic figure. His influence on social and economic change is limited by the customs and assumptions of the society of which he is part. When it is ready for his actions, then he succeeds; not before.

IV

This brief introductory essay has outlined some of the problems encountered in discussions about entrepreneurship. Firm answers are few, although there is no disagreement about the importance

---

[1] For the background see M. Gray, *The Highland Economy 1750–1850* 1957).

of the subject. Any understanding of economic development, in history as in theory, must take full account of the phenomenon. To explain the facets, the divergences and the discontinuities of economic change in so many different societies a sound appreciation of the significance and complex nature of entrepreneurship is essential. To take but one example any analysis of economic development in late nineteenth-century France and Britain must rely upon an acceptable explanation of why businessmen in both countries behaved in the ways they did.[1] Of course it is a wide-ranging subject in which questions far outnumber satisfactory answers. Perhaps this was the main conclusion of the Research Centre in Entrepreneurial History established at Harvard in 1948. One Fellow at the Centre described their approach—'Almost anything that might conceivably concern a historian or social scientist was possibly relevant. Directly or indirectly, if you were interested in research in the social sciences and had some sense of history, what you were working on probably had something to do with entrepreneurship.'[2] Their search for an adequate theory proved fruitless, but they showed in their research publications, particularly in the journal they produced, that they were opening up the frontiers between disciplines—history, sociology, psychology and economics in the most exciting way. Again the goods were not produced in the form of hard, sound volumes. Yet they gave the whole subject a new breadth, that made economists and historians increasingly uneasy about their mechanistic theories on the one hand and their narrow business histories on the other. Fifteen years later we are no nearer the general theory of entrepreneurship that the Harvard Centre set out to propound at the end of the Second World War. This necessarily makes an introduction of this kind very tentative, yet the great relevance of the subject to all students of the social sciences is unquestioned.

---

[1] See footnotes pp. 20 and 27.
[2] H. G. J. Aiken, *op. cit.*, 8.

I

James Maitland, 8th Earl of Lauderdale, *An Inquiry into the Nature and Origin of Public Wealth*, 1804. pp. 162–71.

There is no part of the capital of a country, that more obviously derives its profit from supplanting a portion of labour that would otherwise be performed by man, or from performing a portion which is beyond the reach of his personal exertion, than that which is vested in machinery. That man uses capital in the form of machinery to supplant labour, is one of the peculiarities and distinguishing features of his character. If it was not for this singular faculty, his efforts to provide for his wants, like those of the other animals, would be bounded by what his hands, his teeth, and his feet, could enable him to accomplish.

That we may perceive how the profit of capital thus employed arises from supplanting labour, let us consider the effect of capital vested in machinery, in that first employment of man, the cultivation of the ground. The moment he places a portion of capital in the acquisition of a spade, one man must obviously, in the course of a day, be able, with his spade, to prepare as much land for receiving feed, as fifty could, by the use of their nails. Thus, this portion of capital supplants the necessity of the labour of forty-nine men. In the progress of things, a portion of the national capital comes to be invested in a plough; and one man, with his plough, will prepare as much land for the reception of feed as perhaps six could with their spades. Thus, that portion of capital invested in a plough, supplants the necessity either of the labour of five diggers, or of two hundred and ninety-nine men reduced by absolute want of capital to use their nails . . .

The small profit which the proprietors of machinery generally acquire, when compared with the wages of labour, which the machine supplants, may perhaps create a suspicion of the rectitude of this opinion. Some fire engines, for instance, draw more water from a coal-pit in one day, than could be conveyed on the shoulders of three hundred men, even assisted by the machinery of buckets; and a fire engine undoubtedly performs its labour at a much smaller expense than the amount of the wages of those whose labour it thus supplants. This is, in truth, the case with all machinery. All machines must execute the labour, that was antecedently performed, at a cheaper rate than it could be done by the hand of man; otherwise they would inevitably share the fate of the supposed stocking-loom which could manufacture only one pair of stockings in three days, and be laid aside as useless.

The actual profit drawn for the use of any machine, when universally adopted, must be regulated on the same principle with the hire of a field, or the payment of an artist, or the price of any other commodity; that is, by the proportion betwixt the quantity of machines that can be easily procured, and the demand for them. But that the profit of stock employed in machinery is paid out of a fund that would otherwise be destined to pay the wages of the labour it supplants, is evident; because, if the proprietors of all the capital so employed, would combine to charge a greater sum for the use of the machines than the wages of the labour supplanted, they would be instantly set aside, and the same portion of the revenue of the nation again employed in the payment of wages, that was so directed before the machines were invented.

The case of a patent, or exclusive privilege of the use of a machine usually granted, as the law of England now permits, for fourteen years, to reward an ingenious invention, will tend further to illustrate this.

If such a privilege is given for the invention of a machine, which performs, by the labour of one man, a quantity of work that used to take the labour of four; as the possession of the exclusive privilege prevents any competition in doing the work, but what proceeds from the labour of the four workmen, their wages, as long as the patent continues, must obviously form the measure of the patentee's charge; that is, to secure employment, he has only to charge a little less than the wages of the labour which the machine supplants. But when the patent expires, other machines of the same nature are brought into competition; and then his charge must be regulated on the same principle as every other, according to the abundance of machines, or, (what is the same thing), according to the facility of procuring machines in proportion to the demand for them. This alteration, however, in the rule of charging, does not prevent the profit of the machine being received out of a fund of the same nature of that which it was paid from before the expiration of the patent; to wit, from a part of the revenue of the country, destined, antecedent to the invention of the machine, to pay the wages of the labour it supplants.

Though, in confirmation of this opinion, it is impossible to cite the theory of any learned author who has treated of political economy, it has, however, in its favour, what is perhaps fully better; it derives ample testimony of its truth from the conduct of the unlettered manufacturers themselves, as is sufficiently evinced by the riots that have taken place on the introduction of various pieces of machinery, and particularly at the time the ingenious machines for carding and spinning were first set a-going.

II

J. Rae, *New Principles of Political Economy*, 1834, reprinted as *The Sociological Theory of Capital*, ed. C. W. Mixter, 1905.

It is only when some great and striking improvement issues from the exertions of the inventive power, that we in general attend to its effects. Every one readily grants, that, but for the invention of the steam engine, the capital of Great Britain would want much of its present vast amount. We perceive not so readily the numerous small improvements, which have been gradually, from year to year, spreading themselves through every department of the national industry. But, though not so palpably forced on our observation, we pass them by, they nevertheless exist, and sufficiently account for the manner in which the national capital has been augmenting, by being gradually accumulating in them, without the necessity of supposing that it ever has augmented precisely as that of individuals generally does, by a simple multiplication, under the same form, of any or all the items of which its amount was before made up.

Adam Smith himself admits, that a country may come to be fully stocked in proportion to all the business it has to transact, and have as great a quantity of stock employed, in every particular branch, as the nature and extent of the territory will admit. He speaks of Holland also, as a country which had then nearly acquired its full complement of riches; where, in every particular branch of business, there was the greatest quantity of stock that could be employed in it. It would then appear that, even according to him, the principle of individual accumulation, as a means of advancing the national capital, has limits beyond which it cannot pass. The same cannot be said of that increase which is derived from the attainment of those objects at which the inventive faculty aims. Had Holland, sixty years ago, been put in possession of the astonishing improvements in mechanical and manufacturing industry, which since that period, have sprung up in Great

Britain, who can suppose that she would have wanted ability to continue in the successful pursuit of wealth; or, that she would not have started forward with fresh vigor in the career, and advanced in it with greater rapidity than in any former period of her history?

There is no avoiding the admission, that, to every great advance which nations make in the acquisition of wealth, it is necessary that invention leading to improvement should lend its aid; and, granting this, it necessarily follows (as when one cause is discovered sufficient to account for the phenomena, we should confine ourselves to it), that we are not warranted to assume that they make even the smallest sensible progress without the aid of the same faculty.

To this general observation there are only two apparent exceptions. The progress of commerce by the increase of some particular branch of it, or by the opening of fresh branches; and the settlement of new countries.

If these, however, should be esteemed exceptions to the observation with regard to any particular nation or nations, they are extensions of it with regard to all the nations of the earth; implying that the increase of general wealth is connected with the general spread of invention, or inventions, over the world.

III

J. A. Schumpeter, *The Theory of Economic Development*, 1934. pp. 74–83.

The carrying out of new combinations we call "enterprise"; the individuals whose function it is to carry them out we call "entrepreneurs." These concepts are at once broader and narrower than the usual. Broader, because in the first place we call entrepreneurs not only those "independent" businessmen in an exchange economy who are usually so designated, but all who actually fulfil the function by which we define the concept, even if they are, as is becoming the rule, "dependent" employees of a company, like managers, members of boards of directors, and so forth, or even if their actual power to perform the entrepreneurial function has any other foundations, such as the control of a majority of shares. As it is the carrying out of new combinations that constitutes the entrepreneur, it is not necessary that he should be permanently connected with an individual firm; many "financiers," "promotors," and so forth are not, and still they may be entrepreneurs in our sense. On the other hand, our concept is narrower than the traditional one in that it does not include all heads of firms or managers or industrialists who merely may operate an established business, but only those who actually perform that function. Nevertheless I maintain that the above definition does no more than formulate with greater precision what the traditional doctrine really means to convey. In the first place our definition agrees with the usual one on the fundamental point of distinguishing between "entrepreneurs" and "capitalists"— irrespective of whether the latter are regarded as owners of money, claims to money, or material goods. This distinction is common property today and has been so for a considerable time. It also settles the question whether the ordinary shareholder as such is an entrepreneur, and disposes of the conception of the entrepreneur as risk bearer. Furthermore, the ordinary characterisation of the entrepreneur type by such expressions as "initiative," "authority," or "foresight" points entirely in our direction. For there is little scope for such qualities within the routine of the circular flow, and if this had been sharply separated from the occurrence of changes in this routine itself, the emphasis in the definition of the function of entrepreneurs would have been shifted automatically to the latter. Finally there are definitions which we could simply accept. There is in particular the well known one that goes back to J. B. Say: the entrepreneur's function is to combine the productive factors, to bring them together. Since this is a performance of a special kind only when the factors are combined for a first time—while it is merely routine work if done in the course of running a business; this definition coincides with ours . . .

In the general position of the chief of a primitive horde it is difficult to separate the entrepreneurial element from the others. For the same reason most economists up to the time of the younger Mill failed to keep capitalist and entrepreneur distinct because the manufacturer of a hundred years ago was both; and certainly the course of events since then has facilitated the making of this distinction, as the system of land tenure in England has facilitated the distinction between farmer and landowner, while on the Continent this distinction is still occasionally neglected, especially in the case of the peasant who tills his own soil. But in our case there are still more of such difficulties. The entrepreneur of earlier times was not only as a rule the capitalist too, he was also often—as he still is to-day in the case of small concerns—his own technical expert, in so far as a professional specialist was not called in for special cases. Likewise he was (and is) often his own buying and selling agent, the head of his office, his own personnel manager, and sometimes, even though as a rule he of course employed solicitors, his own legal adviser in current affairs. And it was performing some or all of these functions that regularly filled his days. The carrying out of new combinations can no more be a vocation than the making and execution of strategical decisions, although it is this function and not his routine work that charac- terises the military leader. Therefore the entrepreneur's essential function must always appear mixed up with other kinds of activity, which as a rule must be much more conspicuous than the essential one. Hence the Marshallian definition of the entrepreneur, which simply treats the entrepreneurial function as "management" in the widest meaning, will naturally appeal to most of us. We do not accept it, simply because it does not bring out what we consider to be the salient point and the only one which specifically distinguishes entrepreneurial from other activities. Nevertheless there are types—the course of events has evolved them by degrees—which exhibit the entrepreneurial function with particular purity . . . The modern type of "captain of industry" corresponds more closely to what is meant here, especially if one recognises his identity on the one hand with, say, the commercial entrepreneur of twelfth-century Venice—or, among later types, with John Law—and on the other hand with the village potentate who combines with his agriculture and his cattle trade, say, a rural brewery, an hotel, and a store. But whatever the type, everyone is an entrepreneur only when he actually "carries out new combinations," and loses that character as soon as he has built up his business, when he settles down to running it as other people run their businesses. This is the rule, of course, and hence it is just as rare for anyone always to remain an entrepreneur throughout the decades of his active life as it is for a businessman never to have a moment in which he is an entrepreneur, to however modest a degree.

Because being an entrepreneur is not a profession and as a rule not a lasting condition, entrepreneurs do not form a social class in the technical sense, as, for example, landowners or capitalists or workmen do. Of course the entrepreneurial function will lead to certain class positions for the successful entrepreneur and his family. It can also put its stamp on an epoch of social history, can form a style of life, or systems of moral and aesthetic values; but in itself it signifies a class position no more than it presupposes one. And the class position which may be attained is not as such an entrepreneurial position, but is characterised as landowning or capitalist, according to how the proceeds of the enterprise are used. Inheritance of the pecuniary result and of personal qualities may then both keep up this position for more than one generation and make further enterprise easier for descendants, but the function of the entrepreneur itself cannot be inherited, as is shown well enough by the history of manufacturing families.

But now the decisive question arises: why then is the carrying out of new combinations a special process and the object of a special kind of "function"? Every individual carries on his economic affairs as well as he can. To be sure, his own intentions are never realised with ideal perfection, but ultimately his behaviour is moulded by the influence on him of the results of his conduct, so as to fit circumstances which do not as a rule change suddenly. If a business can never be absolutely perfect in any sense, yet it in time approaches a relative perfection having regard to the surrounding world, the social conditions, the knowledge of the time, and the horizon of each individual or each group. New possibilities are continuously being offered by the surrounding world, in particular new discoveries are continuously being added to the existing store of knowledge. Why should not the individual make just as much use of the new possibilities as of the old, and, according to the market position as he understands it, keep pigs instead of cows, or even choose a new crop rotation, if this can be seen to be more advantageous? And what kind of special new phenomena or problems, not to be found in the established circular flow, can arise there?

While in the accustomed circular flow every individual can act promptly and rationally because he is sure of his ground and is supported by the conduct, as adjusted to this circular flow, of all other individuals, who in turn expect the accustomed activity from him, he cannot simply do this when he is confronted by a new task. While in the accustomed channels his own ability and experience suffice for the normal individual, when confronted with innovations he needs guidance. While he swims with the stream in the circular flow which is familiar to him, he swims against the stream if he wishes to change its channel. What was formerly a help becomes a hindrance. What was a familiar datum becomes an unknown. Where the boundaries of routine stop, many people can go no further, and the rest can only do so in a highly variable manner ... Therefore, in describing the circular flow one must treat combinations of means of production (the production-functions) as data, like natural possibilities and admit only small variations at the margins, such as every individual can accomplish by adapting himself to changes in his economic environment, without materially deviating from familiar lines.

Therefore, too, the carrying out of new combinations is a special function, and the privilege of a type of people who are much less numerous than all those who have the "objective" possibility of doing it. Therefore, finally, entrepreneurs are a special type, and their behaviour a special problem, the motive power of a great number of significant phenomena. Hence, our position may be characterised by three corresponding pairs of opposites. First, by the opposition of two real processes: the circular flow or the tendency towards equilibrium on the one hand, a change in the channels of economic routine or a spontaneous change in the economic data arising from within the system on the other. Secondly, by the opposition of two theoretical *apparatuses*: statics and dynamics. Thirdly, by the opposition of two types of conduct, which, following reality, we can picture as two types of individuals: mere managers and entrepreneurs. And therefore the "best method" of producing in the theoretical sense is to be conceived as "the most advantageous among the methods which have been empirically tested and become familiar." But it is not the "best" of the methods "possible" at the time. If one does not make this distinction, the concept becomes meaningless and precisely those problems remain unsolved which our interpretation is meant to provide for.

IV

In January 1777 I was sent to Hipperholme which was then a good classical school, where I remained a year and a half, and after an interval of half a year, I went to Mr. Astley of Dronfield in Derbyshire where I staid a year and a half. Mr. Astley was not a man of much learning or strength of understanding, but a very amiable man, and his plan of instruction was well calculated for giving a taste for general knowledge and literature. I afterwards learnt French and Merchants accounts at Leeds and was taken into my Father's business in March 1782. The next year my Father built a new house and warehouse in Millhill of the overlooking of which I had the principal share, which gave me a taste for building that I shall always retain. He removed to it in 1784 and carried on there the wholesale linen business, and in 1785 Samuel Fenton was taken in as a partner with a quarter share.

In December 1787 my Father died of a paralytic or appoplectic stroke, deservedly lamented by all who knew him. He was not eminent for abilities or mental acquirments, but for kindness and generosity to all with whom he was connected, and a conscientious desire to do his duty without regard to his private interest, he had few who were his equals. He was only 57 when he died; he was a stout man, had lived a very regular life, and had scarcely ever suffered from any illness.

My Grandfather was a respectable country gentleman who lived upon his own estate at Yeadon, which he left to his eldest son, and having a numerous family, the fortunes of the younger children were small.

My Father was brought up to trade, and began the world with £200, the greatest part of which he lost in a few months, by some linens which were lost at sea. This however did not abate the confidence which his former masters, Mr. Cloudsley and Mr.

Stevenson, reposed in him. They supplied him with capital, and he prospered. I have heard him in after life, relate the account of his loss with pleasurable recollections. His integrity and diligence in business could not fail to increase his property, though he always lived plentifully and hospitably, and did many kindnesses to his relations. Including my mother's original fortune which was an estate worth £1,200, my father was worth about £9,000 when he died.

Had I now been content to go on in the beaten track which my Father had marked out for me, I might probably have passed through life in a quiet regular way, and saved myself many a heart ache.

My Father left no will, and my Mother and I had made no division of the property which with the profits of the trade produced about a thousand pounds a year. This was nearly double our expences, and made a yearly increase that might have satisfied a moderate man; nor was it with the mere desire of getting money, that I entered into more hazardous schemes, but with the ambition of distinguishing myself.

I longed for an employment where there was a field for exertion and improvement, where difficulties were to be encountered, and distinction and riches to be obtained by overcoming them. My attention was accidentally turned to spinning of flax by machinery, it being a thing much wished for by the linen manufacturers. The immense profits which had been made by cotton spinning had attracted general attention to mechanical improvements and it might be hoped that flax spinning, if practicable, would be equally advantageous. It would be a new business, where there would be few competitors, and was much wanted for the linen manufacture of this country. My partner S. Fenton was as eager to undertake it as myself, and in partnership with Ralph Dearlove of Knaresborough a linen manufacturer of great probity and good sense, we took a small water mill at Scotland four miles from Leeds, and worked some machinery on the patent plan of Kendrew and Co. This did not answer, and we tried experiments, and took out a patent for a plan of Mathew Murray's our principal mechanic and in 1791 we built a mill at Leeds . . .

V

G. F. French, *Life and Times of Samuel Crompton*, 1859. pp. 92–7.

It thus appears that this meritorious but unfortunate man (Samuel Crompton)—in utter despair of advancing his own position in life by the aid of his transcendent invention, which while bringing fortunes to hundreds, bread to thousands, and increased comfort to millions round about him, left him and his family nevertheless in comparative poverty—was compelled to renounce the use of his mules, and to betake himself to his original occupation of weaving, or at least to spin only such yarn as he could employ in his own looms as a small manufacturer. This bitter necessity must have been doubly painful to him, as it occurred about the same time that David Dale of Lanark first employed water power to turn the mule frames, thus greatly increasing their importance and value; and also by the fact that Sir Richard Arkwright, who died soon after, left enormous wealth in land, money, mills and machinery to his two children.

Let us for a moment contrast the characters and the fortunes of these two remarkable Bolton men. Crompton's start in life was made from a much more favourable position than Arkwright's. A carefully-nurtured only son, his early education was excellent, and during his long life he persevered in acquiring knowledge. By continued self-education, based upon his excellent school tuition under Barlow, he had made himself conversant with algebra and trigonometry. He was a good mathematician, and so expert in arithmetical calculations as to be frequently consulted in disputes on such matters. He was an accomplished musician, with much knowledge of the science and great practical skill in playing on various instruments; Handel and Corelli were his favourite composers, and his musical friends so well knew his power as a timeist that they chose him leader of their concerts and practice-meetings. Next to music he delighted in mechanics, and spent much time in inventing and constructing with his own hands implements for his trade, and even articles of domestic furniture. He took much pleasure in the practice of his own art, and had an honourable pride in spinning the finest yarn and weaving the most delicate muslins in the trade. No man however can excel in all things; and it was Mr. Crompton's misfortune to undervalue and disregard that practical knowledge of the world and of men which is essentially necessary for success in any business. This rendered him quite unable to dispose of his yarn and muslins when he had made them, however great their intrinsic value. His naturally shy disposition moreover had been increased and his temper injured by the cruel injustice which had so frequently blighted his hopes when in the bud. This peculiarity of character may be best understood from his own words: "I found to my sorrow I was not calculated to contend with men of the world; neither did I know there was such a thing as protection for me on earth! I found I was as unfit for the task that was before me as a child of two years old to contend with a disciplined army." And such was indeed the fact. When he attended the Manchester Exchange to sell his yarns or muslins, and any rough-and-ready manufacturer ventured to offer him a less price than he had asked, he would invariably wrap up his samples, put them into his pocket, and quietly walk away. He was never either in want or in debt. Frugality was the custom of the time, and he practised it faithfully in his own person and taught it to his family. Utterly averse to speculation, he was well content with a moderate and regular profit in his business transactions when he could obtain it.

How different the character and the career of Sir Richard Arkwright. The thirteenth child of a family steeped to the lips in poverty, he was turned into the world without education, which in after life he never found time to acquire. Trained to a servile handicraft, and without a shilling of capital, the position from which he raised his fortunes had not one of the advantages enjoyed by Crompton; but to compensate for this he possessed an indomitable energy of purpose which no obstacle could success-fully oppose, a bronzed assurance that enabled him unabashed to meet and to thrust aside either circumstances or men when they stood in his way, an unscrupulous hand to grasp and appropriate the ideas and immatured inventions of others, a rude health that enabled him to work or travel when others slept, and an undaunted spirit for speculation, prepared to accept success or failure without any visible effect on his mind or temper. Thus their functions and career in life were singularly different, while both were benefactors to the human race . . .

VI

J. Meteyard, *Life and Works of Josiah Wedgwood*, 1865, Vol. 1.
pp. 224, 229–34, 260–2.

For whatever was the perfection, in some respects, of his physical
and consequently his mental and moral heritage, something was
certainly due to training and example. He had undoubtedly a
simple, peaceful home, in which, if there was no luxury, there was
no poverty or vice. Most of those who were allied to him had
happily to work for their daily bread; there was the necessity for,
and the practice of, frugality and industry; and the influences
around him were altogether of that homely, practical and earnest
description which have moulded the character of some of our
greatest men . . .

The remainder of his apprenticeship, from his sixteenth to his
nineteenth year, embraced that critical passage from youth to
early manhood, when the mental and the moral characteristics so
strongly indicate themselves. And in this case they were of the
highest kind: no tavern-hunting, no brawling, no vice of other
kinds, but a steady attention to the duties before him, and a
determinate self-culture. The exordium in the quaintly-worded
indenture was no mere dead letter; it was vital, and bore as noble
fruit as his worthy mother could desire. Probably, at the time, this
augmentation of his early infirmity was looked upon as a great
misfortune by himself and his friends. It cut him off, as perhaps
they thought, from an active career, whilst in reality it involved
the whole measure of a philosophic and ideal conception of the
potter's art—a blending of utility and beauty, which, reproducing
the truth and grace of the classic ages, showed that such are
eternal in principle, and need only the spirit of genius to again
and again evoke them, under formulas and constructions adapted
to a newer age. The new, in this case, and the old are one. Judging
from what we may call the physiology of mental evolutions, it is
probable that the young man suffered, in this passage of his life,

from the depressions and conflicts with self, which all those who aspire to do their work after the highest type to be conceived of it, only know too well: those sinkings of the heart at shortcomings, those moments when the battle seems too long and too weary; those periods of deep self-humiliation, when the result of our toil is so poor in fulfilment, and falls so immeasurably short of our ideal. Happy for us is it, and the cause of truth we serve, let the formula be what it may, if, like the young man Josiah Wedgwood, we begin the conflict anew; for the next step is still stronger, and involves a nearer approach to our ideal. This humility of spirit is a primary element of progress; for the conception of our ignorance includes the desire to learn; and Josiah Wedgwood must have passed through these necessary throes of self-culture, though the equable character of his mind, and his naturally cheerful temper, may have made these conflicts but little to be observed by those around him . . .

To this period we may also assign his earliest attempts in respect to that more ornamental class of small wares in the manufacture of which his relative Dr. Thomas Wedgwood had so excelled. This brought him into the track of experiment and analysis; for though the different clays and metallic oxides necessary to the imitation of agate, marble, melon, tortoiseshell, and other natural bodies, were well known in all the best potworks of the time, his mind was far too original to rest satisfied, even at this early date, in simply following in the mere path of other men's discoveries. By repeated trials, he succeeded in varying the agate ware into an excellent imitation of porphyry—an effect previously attempted, but never so successfully. With these two bodies he made knife-hafts and snuffboxes for the cutlers and hardwaremen of Sheffield and Birmingham; and for the disposal of these, it is said, he paid his first visit to the latter place in 1748, being then in his eighteenth year. For pickle-leaves, small dishes for confections, and other d'oeuvres as they were then styled, he sought assistance from the best mould-makers; and with the care thus bestowed, and the usual glaze of lead ore and flint, the results were often admirable . . . He [Thomas Wedgwood] had not the least sympathy with his young brother's ardent love for their joint art, but, on the contrary, was constantly reproving him for giving way to what he considered an idle and unprofitable curiosity in making experiments and trying new processes, and earnestly counselled him not to risk his future prosperity by indulging his imagination in forming new schemes and endless illusive projects.

Undaunted by these reiterated homilies of self-satisfied ignorance, young Wedgwood, upon the close of his apprenticeship, proposed to become his brother's partner, and as such push on their trade, as well as introduce many necessary reforms in their manufacturing processes and working establishment. But Thomas Wedgwood would not consent: he was wedded to his own methods of business, and dreaded perhaps the diminution of his own authority were his brother's active spirit of industry and superior intellect suffered to gain the ascendant . . .

Accordingly, some time early in the year 1751 or 1752, the young man took upon himself the management of Alder's potwork, at probably a very low salary, judging it by the sums then paid to modellers and other high-class workmen by the masterpotters, or to men like Brindley for engineering work of a most complicated kind. But it was soon seen that a master-hand had come amongst them. Even the blue-scratched and common wares began to a show a density of body, a clearness of glaze, and an improvement in form. The barbarous art which adorned them also betokened a change for the better. Sales increased; and as to productions of a higher class of ware, such as small articles for ornamental and useful purposes, they were something new to the works, and found ready purchasers in Birmingham, Manchester, and elsewhere. The cupidity of Harrison and his partner was excited. They urged the young man to fresh exertions in this direction, without increasing his share in the profits; whilst personally he was hindered in many ways by their ignorance, interference, and by the absence of those necessaries without which no improvement in an art or a science can be carried onwards . . .

His capital was also limited: till it increased, any great extension of his trade either through the introduction of new kinds of ware, new designs, or the employment of a large body of workmen, was impossible. The latter were at first few in number, and he had even these, as it were, to educate to his hand, for the methods then in use were, generally speaking, of the most slovenly description; but his sound judgment led him, when choice was possible, to select men who ultimately did the greatest justice to his instructions, and whose services were life-long. This keen insight into character was one of Josiah Wedgwood's idiosyncrasies; and it helped him as much in the beginning as in the after organisation of his great works. At this date Mr. Wedgwood made most of his own models, prepared his mixtures, superintended the firing processes, and for a short period was his own clerk and warehouseman. He was thus, so far as his health permitted, incessantly employed in the various departments of his small pot-work . . .

His first step in this business of extension and improvement was to hire some more hovels and working sheds in close vicinity to the Ivy House; his next, to considerably increase his body of workmen. To each of these he assigned a certain branch in his manufacture; it being still the ordinary custom for the journeymen potters to pass from one kind of labour to another, just as impulse or convenience prompted, and this without reference to either the necessities of the moment or their master's interest. Wedgwood had long observed the evils of this system—the idle, slovenly, and irregular habits it begot in the workmen, and the loss of time and waste of efficiency in regard to productive results. Whilst his brother's apprentice, and still very young, he had, as we have seen, tried to modify somewhat this old system of things; and now that he was thoroughly his own master he resolved that, so far as he was concerned, they should no longer exist. At first he met with much sullen opposition, often amounting to an insubordination that necessitated immediate dismissal; but by firmness, patience, and great kindness he succeeded, in a comparatively short time, in bringing his manufactory into efficient order. His men found that it was much better to obey than to oppose; and that the regulations that they had at first clamoured against facilitated their labour to a surprising degree.

The manufacture of white ware, relief tiles, and small ornamental articles, was carried on at the new works. But Wedgwood saw clearly that it was not these classes of ware which would either open or secure a new and great market. What was wanting was a ware of a superior description, so excellent in all respects as to be suited to the tables of the upper classes; and which, when

improvements and facility in production should enable the manufacturer to sell it at a cheaper rate, might reach those of the
middle classes. He had for a considerable period, as we have seen,
turned his attention towards the improvement of the ordinary
cream-coloured ware, manufactured at various pot-works in
Burslem and its neighbourhood. But his experiments had been
desultory; rather directed to future purposes than immediate
results. He now, however, concentrated all his energies for a
period in this one direction. Every essential of body, glaze, form,
and ornament was alike the object of his care. But through the
various necessary processes his patience was often sorely tried; his
repeated failures most disheartening. One kiln after another was
pulled down in order to correct some defect, or effect some
necessary improvement. His losses from this source alone were at
this period very heavy, and the ware itself was often destroyed
before he could bring his firing processes to the requisite degree
of perfection. His chemical combinations often baffled him; and
his experiments both in body and glaze would, after the greatest
pains, turn out entire failures. Yet, unwearied and indomitable in
spirit, he persevered, and success came. He had to invent, and, if
not that, to improve almost every tool, instrument, and apparatus;
and to seek for smiths and machinists to work under his guidance.
Lathes, whirlers, punches, gravers, models, moulds, drying-pans,
and many other things were all variously improved. He often
passed the whole day at the bench beside his men, and in many
cases instructed them individually. The first pattern of each
original piece he almost always made himself; and though no
great draughtsman, the enamellers could work from his designs.

From this course of preparative work he rarely rested. He spent
the evenings and a large part of each night in making chemical
experiments, in contriving instruments and tools to effect some
novel process, in modelling, in sketching ornaments and patterns,
or otherwise preparing for the business of the succeeding day. So
much hold did many of these inventions take upon his mind as to
deprive him of sleep for nights together; and rest rarely came till
he had satisfied his stern will and fastidious taste in relation to the
object he had in view.

VII

A. H. John (ed.), *The Walker Family Iron Founders and Lead Manufacturers 1741–1893*, The Council for the Preservation of Business Archives, 1951. pp. 1–19.

1741

After some tryal made in Foundering, by Aaron Walker and John Crawshaw, in potts, with but bad success, in Abram. Booth's Smithey, in Oughty-bridge Lane, in the spring of the year 1741.[1]

In or about October or November of the same year, Saml. and Aaron Walker built an Air Furnace in the old nailor's smithey, on the backside of Saml. Walker's cottage at Grenoside, making some small addition thereto, and another little hutt or two, slating with sods, &c., with a small Garth walled in: and after rebuilding the chimney or stacks once, and the furnace once or more, begun to proceed a little, Saml. Walker teaching the school at Grenoside, and Aaron Walker making nails and mowing and shearing, &c., part of his time.

One Saml. Saint, who was slitting steel at Sheffield, who had sometime before worked a little in the foundry way, came and assisted at one small casting of bushes,[2] which was all the hands that had any experience that was imploy'd for near 12 years.

NOVEMBER 1742

We had made goods, as near as we could guess, to the amount of about Five Tons.

---

[1] The source of these early business journals is a complicated one. They were compiled by A. O. Walker in 1878–9 and are based substantially upon the journals of his forelders, particularly Samuel Walker (1715–82), one of three brothers who founded the firm. Unfortunately these journals which Walker consulted in the 1870's no longer survive. See A. H. John's introduction.—Eds.

[2] The iron linings for wooden hubs of cart wheels.

NOVEMBER 1743

This year we made goods to the amount of about Ten Tons. Aaron Walker now begun to be pretty much imploy'd and had 4 shillings a week to live upon, and the rest of his time or wage balanced what time Saml. Walker could spare from the school.

We also imploy'd John Crawshaw as much as we could at 12 pence per day.

NOVEMBER 1744

This year we made goods to the amot. of 31½ tons.

Pulled down the old smithey and hutts to ye ground, and built a new Foundry wth. 2 air furnaces and a smithey to it, and enlarged and walled the Garth or Fould Stead.

NOVEMBER 1745

This year we made about 39 tons of castings; and, as we had occasion, took in raw hands, such as nailors, husbandmen, &c.

This year Saml. Walker, finding business increase, was obliged to give up his school, and built himself a house at the end of the old cottage, then thought he was fixed for life; then we allowed ourselves ten shilling a-week each for wages to maintain our families.

NOVEMBER 1746

This year we made 63½ tons of castings; and now, a valuation being made of the effects, the capital

amounted to	£400 0 0
Jonathan Walker put into stock	100 0 0
John Crawshaw do	50 0 0
Saml. Walker added	50 0 0
Which made the capital	£600 0 0

And though S. Walker, the year before, thought himself so well settled, begun to see ye disadvantage of being so far from ye navigable river, and with a deal of trouble prevailed to have a beginning at Masborough, near Rotherham, where we built a casting-house, with two air furnaces and a smithey adjoining; and Aaron remooved from Grenoside to a little house of Mrs. Cotterel's, opposite her house. . .

NOVEMBER 1747

This year we made 96 tons of castings, and we supposed ye value of ye capital £900 0 0

In this year we built Aaron Walker a house by the Foundry, at Masbro'.

NOVEMBER 1748

This year we made 110 tons of castings, and supposed the value of the capital then £1,300 0 0

We built one bay for a warehouse at the end of the foundry at Grennoside, fenced Hind's Farm (at the hill-top) round, and repaired the housing, &c., belonging it.

This year Saml. Walker and Mr. Jno. Booth built the steel furnace at Masbro': the land was purchased of Benjamin Drabble.

NOVEMBER 1749

This year we made 129 tons of castings, and supposed the value of the capital £1,800 0 0

Built a furnace to cast pots in, and a barn adjoining, opposite Aaron Walker's house at Masbro', and a little warehouse adjoining the end of his house; a little compting-house and a small place to cast brass in; and a barn at the foundry at Grennoside.

Also Mr. Booth and S. Walker built a dwelling-house and barn adjoining, above the steel furnace, and S. Walker came the beginning of this month (Novr.) to live there.

[The entries continue in much the same vein, showing the way in which some additions were made to the plant every year, until 1756 when there is a note that the first dividend—of £140—was taken. Even then, although the stock was valued at £6,800, Samuel Walker wrote, 'I hope the Forge etc. may answer it.' Throughout the eighteenth century the firm distributed a small proportion of its profits and by the standards of the day it built up a very appreciable capital through the assiduous ploughback of profits. A sample of entries for subsequent years show these trends very clearly.—Eds.]

NOVEMBER 1758

This year we made 284¼ tons of castings, and supposed the nett stock, (after we have divided £140)   £8,500 0 0

Built a tin-house at ye forge; corn chambers with cart-houses under, also a hay-loft with cart-house under, and 2 cow-houses, in the Yellands.

At ye Holmes, rebuilt the slitting and rolling mill, with ye tin house and smithey adjoining. Also the blast furnace, bellows, and casting-house, and made a navigable cutt thence to near the Eccles, with the floodgates going into ye Eccles Cutt; made a bridge from ye Holmes Green into Finches' Close, and one bridge over the cutt going into the Holmes Lane and 3 over the goit; made the dam and by-wash to the mill, and laid a pentrough ready for a grinding mill; deepened and widened the goit from the Works up to Jordan dam, and built 3 dwelling-houses, 2 cow-houses, and a cart-house at the Holmes; besides very great trouble and expence in opening the Iron-stone Works and Colliery, and made almost incredible improvements in the road to the Holmes from Masbro and Kimberworth, and in ye Lanes towards Tinsley, and made very great improovmt. in ye land also.

GLORIA DEO.

N.B. Some of the above buildings were not quite compleated at the end of this year, but was soon after quite finished.

NOVEMBER 1763

This year we made 448½ tons of castings, and supposed the valuation of the nett stock, after taking out £350 for a dividend, and other deductions, to be £15,200 0 0

This year the Works turned out very well, supposed £3,000 but deducted £1,300 for law expences, losses, the above dividend, interest of money, clark's wages, &c., and supposed to have added to the capital £1,700.

This year we built Thribrough Forge, and 4 dwelling-houses, carpenter and smith's shops, charcoal yard, and other necessaries there. Built a stable and 2 large workshops or smitheys in ye Yellands, built a new nealing room[1] at the Holms Mills; built an additional piece to the scrap house at Rotherham Forge.

1 MAY 1769

We now suppose the clear value of the Company's effects to be £42,500, besides £1,400, which has been divided this year.

From 27th Novr. 1768, to 27th Novr. 1769, castings made as Day Book, 580 tons, 3 ct., 0 s., 5 lb. besides 80 tons ballast; of the above, there was 82 tons, 17 ct., 2 s., 8lb. sad irons.

Built this year at Thribergh Mill two new dwelling-houses; at Masbrough—a new warehouse opposite the stables, a parlour for Matt. Bailey, and a parlour and chamber for J. Smith, with a little house by Smith's house; S.W. house finish'd, with a brew-house, garden walls, and other out-conveniences; and a little parlour rebuilt, with a chamber over it, for A.W. At the Holmes—rebuilt the Loam House, making it twice as big as it was; a large cart-house, and an additional part to the new tin-house.

1 MAY 1775

We now suppose the Company's effects to be £58,500; tho' there have been great losses by J.W., &c., the profits of the Forges, Mills, &c., have been large.

---

[1] An annealing room—used in the manufacture of tinplate.

From Novr. 27th, 1774, to Novr. 24th, 1775, castings made 694 tons, 12 ct., 5 s., 12 lb.; of which were sad irons 91 tons, 7 ct., 1 s., 13 lb.—

Of which were sent to Ldn. — 58 tons, 1 ct., 7 s., 5 lb.
To other places   — 33   5   2   8

            ——————————————
            91   7   1   13
            ——————————————

Debentures for Guns rec'd this year (viz. to Novr. 1775) 40 tons. 16 ct., 6 s., 11 lb.

1 MAY 1777

We now suppose the Company's effects to be £102,500, tho' this may be thot. too high; but when we consider the quantity of Guns made this year, and the good success therein, and the interest for the money lent, &c., there seems good reason for the above supposition. . .

This year we were bereaved of our partner Aa. Walker, who died in January, after a life of much industry. He had the internal management of the casting and steel trade, in which he certainly exhibited more ingenuity than patience. He left a widow, "Rhoda"; a son "John", married to a soldier's wife; a daughter, "Hannah", married to Mr. Jno. Pearson, of Leeds, Wine Mercht. He was buried in the Chapel Yard, over which a Monument is erected.

1 MAY 1782

Suppos'd value of Capital 1st May 1781, brot. forward   £110,000
Add to the above the suppos'd increase since 1st May
                    1781 to 1st May 1782   18,000
                                        —————————
                                        £128,000
            Divided this 1st May 1782   28,000
                                        —————————
                    Company's capital   £100,000
                                        —————————

Castings made (exclusive of Guns) from Novr. 1781 to Novr. 1782 as Day Book, 859 tons, 14 ct., 4 s., 9 lb., of which were sad irons—

To London —	42 tons,	18 ct.,	4 s.,	6 lb.
To Country —	15	19	6	6
Total	58	18	2	12

Debentures for Guns dated within the above yr.

	1039	9	1	7
Add the castings from above	859	14	4	9
Total of castings	1899	3	6	2

One the 12th of May this Concern suffer'd an irreparable loss in the death of the first partner in the Firm, SAMUEL WALKER, who has left a widow, four sons, and three daughters. It is unnecessary to say what obligations mankind in general, and this partnership in particular, are under to that integrity, industry, foresight, and perseverance, which appeared in all his actions.

BUILDINGS, &C. 1782

About Holme—Built new large stables for 10 horses, adjoining the compting house; built a new shed for our sawyers in the Yellands, 20 yards long, and made good commodious pits under it. Thribro' Forge—Widen'd the race, put in a new sheel, put up a pair of cillender bellows, all at the North Finery, and made an addition to the building, put up a new chaffing wheel; built a new compting house at the top of the steps.

Rothm. Forge—Lined the balling hamr. beams, and made other repairs.

Masbro'—Built new stables for 4 horses, coach-house, &c.; made many alterations in the inside of the house, in and about the court, fold, &c., to accommodate Mrs. W.

Jordan Dam—Pitched 16 or 18 yards in length of the Wear, and built a new wall at this end to support the bank. The goit has had usual repairs.

Holmes—Made various alterations and improvements at the Hall to sute Mr. S.W. at his cost. Took the roof off the old furnace casting house, raised the walls about 6 ft.; put on a new roof, erected a new crane and a new cast-metal spur wheel; built a new settling house in addition to the old one; enlarged the Bridghouse floor over the old wheel.

Boring House at bottom of Kettle Croft—Took out the wheel and built new substantial ashler walls on each side the goit.

Fire Engine completed to blow out three furnaces, and began to work in September.

VIII

R. G. Wilson, The Fortunes of a Leeds Merchant House, 1780–1820, *Business History* IX, 1967. pp. 80–4.

Since 1810, the firm had done well and weathered the depression of 1810–12 with ease. During 1811 the partners had begun manufacturing their own cloth, woollens, Rhodes proudly claimed, of 'super-excellent qualities'.[1] The factory was extensive, especially in machine-dressing, a brave departure at a time when the cloth-dressers' combinations had had considerable success in the Leeds area in resisting the installations of gig-mills. Glover, who had never seen the establishment, received the following glowing description from his senior partner, 'I have built a little Town at Woodhouse Carr for the convenience of Business. We manufacture about 60 Ends of Cloth weekly, we dress all by machinery and finish all our own Stuffs, and are going to dye all our own cloths, when you will wonder how we have got such buildings together, but we have worked hard the last four years and have been fortunate'. Certainly, 1813 had been a wonderful year for the firm in Leeds. As Rhodes wrote to Rio on 6 November, 'We are almost worked to death we have so much Business, we are sought from every Quarter . . . we are becoming a House of not little consequence in this country.' Three days later he continued in the same jubilant strain, 'We have wonderful success in Business you may form some idea how we have worked

---

[1] Abraham Rhodes and his brothers had made great fortunes in the Leeds cloth export trade since the 1780's. In 1810 he had formed a new partnership with his brother William Rhodes (who represented the firm in the United States), Henry Glover, the erratic junior partner who conducted their South American trade from Rio de Janeiro and Thomas Clapham, a member of an old merchant family in Leeds who had recently married Glover's sister. In 1811 they began to manufacture cloth themselves, although the majority of cloth they sold was still principally bought from other clothiers and manufacturers in and around Leeds.—Eds.

lately when we tell you that our Invoices amounted to £20,000 from October to November 4 last'.

With the coming of the New Year, however, a familiar ominous tone crept into the correspondence. Glover had been remiss in securing bills of payment; the firm was 'Poverty struck after twelve months of Plenty'. Admittedly, Glover's waywardness was not the sole cause of the firm's difficulties. Returns were slow from all quarters. Moreover William Rhodes had recently died in New York, and £5,000 was required immediately for his widow, apart from his capital which would eventually be withdrawn. And the price of cheap woollens had advanced some 50 percent during 1812 'becoming so scarce hardly any to be had for money'.

Nevertheless, Henry Glover's hesitancy to make quick returns to Leeds seriously aggravated Rhodes' predicament. The latter plainly stated the gravity of the situation in February, 'You should let us have £30,000 with all speed we stand in a need of every shilling of it'. Meanwhile Glover had become involved in a new venture which admitted little consideration for the partners' plight at home. Out of his latest scheme evolved one of the strangest triangular trades on record. He had begun to ship jerked beef from Rio to Havanna, where coffee and sugar were taken on board for Gibraltar. For the return voyage the ships were loaded with wine for Brazil . . .

The cumulative impact of Glover's hazardous speculation on the firm, and his abrogation of every tenet of the old mercantile faith, is graphically told in the correspondence. Even without his risky undertaking, the firm had sufficient problems during 1814. Trade with the United States was at a complete standstill; the Portuguese market was very flat, and the German one was recovering only slowly. Moreover the price of woollens was so high in spring that speculation could not lightly be undertaken. Again the immediate problems, however, were those of returns and ready cash. No less than £15,000 was due from the Portuguese market alone, and William Rhodes' executors were now pressing for £10,000. In a pleading letter Rhodes laid out the firm's plight at length, 'We have got into such a way of Business so accustomed to pay for every Article on its being delivered at our warehouse, that it cuts us to the very soul, to be incapacitated to continue the Practice, reflect for a moment that for the last 12 months we have drawn upon our Bankers after the rate of £12,000 per month, which sums up very fast in our Bankers Books against us, when there is a stoppage of remittances to place on the other side, and except the £4,000 we have drawn upon you we have not had a farthing on account of any goods sent you in 1813. We open our hearts and tell you our Sorrows, comfort and relieve them'.

When all went well elsewhere, the firm was able to absorb Glover's follies in Brazil, now, when the state of economic activity was again falling, it could no longer digest his shortcomings. The desperate plea for money was renewed in August. Rhodes disclosed that they owed the Bank £22,000. As he pointed out, the debt could easily be wiped out were Glover prepared to repay even half the £45,000 he owed the firm in Leeds. In the same month Thomas Clapham, who very seldom wrote to Glover, added his stern word to the renewed bombardment of the recalcitrant partner. Believing that the best psychological approach to spur Glover into action was a glowing account of the firm's successes, he penned a letter which made impressive reading: 'The last four years up the 5th April we made a profit of about £60,000, we observe you have made a profit of £18,000 there are not many houses in Leeds can say so much'. Things look so black that the Leeds partners were making plans for the dissolution of the partnership two years ahead. They wanted Glover to liquidate his debts and return, 'above all we recommend to you get quit of your shipping in which as partners we entirely disapprove'. They pointed out that the exchange rates were so favourable that he would be well-advised to turn all his stocks into bills which were themselves returning a twenty per cent profit in October and November.

Still no money came. Glover had even stopped replying to letters. In spring 1815, with the resumption of trade with the United States, the firm required every penny it could lay its hands on. By June, prospects in America were so favourable that Rhodes wrote 'if we had £30,000 more capital we would employ it'. Profits were not large, but their connections in the United States were very reliable, and the amount of business done was so considerable that the American trade was extremely remunerative. Unfortunately Glover's wild schemes in Brazil were being reported back to Leeds, giving the firm a thoroughly bad name throughout the West Riding. The partners were at a loss what to do: in July 1815, Rhodes was desperately pleading, 'a change of scenery will do you much good, if you come amongst us I flatter myself you will be more happy than remaining at Rio . . . the mind requires relief and a change'.

Of the £30,000 that the firm had demanded from Glover in January, not a penny had been forthcoming. Therefore in September, Rhodes and Clapham had been forced to go to their bankers for an extra-ordinary advance of £15,000 above their usual allowance in order to carry through their American orders. Export merchants in the woollen trade required frequent advances to tide over their payments to the manufacturers before their foreign remittances became due, and the Leeds banks had largely grown by providing such facilities. Naturally their willingness to make these short-term loans depended entirely on the merchants' word and reputation. The name of the Rhodes had now sunk so low that the Union Bank's partners, close relatives of Abraham Rhodes, consented to the advance only on a written assurance that the £30,000 that Glover had promised would be paid to them within six months. Glover quickly remitted £10,000; but then to cover the expenses of *Ulysses*, now *en route* to Liverpool, he had drawn upon the firm for £4,000. This transaction placed the two Leeds partners in a very poor light with the Bank, 'they now believe it (the promise to pay into their account Glover's outstanding £30,000) was a trick to get them to make heavy advances for us and that in fact you have nothing to send us *indeed* our Bankers don't hesitate telling us your concern at Rio is a very ruinous one and the world even goes further it is reported that the concern at Rio is already ruined, and that you will bring this concern also to the same state'. The colossal endeavour of the past six years was crumbling. Rhodes had built the firm up until it had 'become almost one of the first in this town', and yet as he sadly commented, 'it will be useless for us to rise early and work late to procure a subsistence for ourselves if we and they are to be brought to Beggary'.

The Leeds partners were now absolutely bent on closing the business in Rio, and on giving up the shipping ventures entirely. Yet how were they to curtail Glover's activities without further risk to the reputation of the firm? As Rhodes confessed, 'We might as well address ourselves to the man in the moon you pay no attention to our requests'. And with a true Yorkshire succinctiness he added, 'You had better do nothing than mischief'. It was infuriating at a time when the firm had excellent prospects in the United States that a good part of their capital should be perilously locked up in Brazil. Clapham believed the firm could achieve an annual turnover of £200,000 by their united exertion. Though every penny that the house received from the United States was immediately paid in, their efforts failed to convince the Bank, and it renewed its pressure. Thomas Clapham gave Glover a full account of the Bank's senior partner's dramatic appearance: 'I was dining with A(braham) R(hodes) after dinner Wm. Brown Partner with our Bankers made his appearance—he accosted us as follows "I dare say I am an unwelcome visitor I am come respecting your account and request it may be immediately discharged, as we plainly see your resources are now what you have led us to expect in Mr Glover's hands, you have accepted now near £5,000 of his Drafts when we were expecting you to pay us in remittances from him only not less than £20,000 though your own proposal was £30,000 had not you deluded us with such a promise we could never have given you credit for the enormous amount that now stands against you".' Brown flatly refused them a further penny in advance. At this critical point the correspondence ends.

The firm's affairs in Rio de Janeiro were wound up during late 1816, and Henry Glover was back in Leeds before Christmas, presumably leaving the final details to his capable assistant Samuel Sykes. Several months earlier, Thomas Clapham had informed his two colleagues that he had found a 'very eligible partnership' with another export house in town. Abraham Rhodes had made it abundantly clear that he wished to rid himself of all association with Glover. There was nothing unusual in the termination of the partnership: indeed there had been a move away from the long inter-family associations which had been common in the quieter days before the upheavals following the American war. What was exceptional was the way the partnership was dissolved.

IX

R. H. Campbell, The Financing of Carron Company, *Business History*, I, 1958. pp. 28–33.

Once he became manager Gascoigne's whole effort was directed towards obtaining financial assistance. The way out was not easy. Few of the partners could help. Those of the Roebuck family who remained partners were either too heavily engaged in other activities or had their resources already strained almost to the limit by commercial failures and bankruptcy so that they were both unable and unwilling to provide further funds. The Cadells, though probably still able to provide help, had not only seen the works grow beyond their original expectations, but had also seen the management transferred to what must have been to them undesirable hands. In any event one of Gascoigne's chief aims was to have them removed completely from the Company just as he had managed to eject John Roebuck. Having by 1769 in large measure succeeded, he was unwilling to prejudice his chances of ultimate success by allowing the family any further interest or influence. The two other partners who might have helped, both of whom would have been acceptable to Gascoigne, were John Adam and the Garbetts. The former, as became evident later, was not in a position to salvage the Company. In any case at that time his family was already committed to large building ventures. The other, and in more normal circumstances the most likely source of funds, was Samuel Garbett, though now only a relatively small shareholder, having transferred four shares to his son, Francis, and one to Gascoigne. The circulation of bills, which Gascoigne had undertaken on Garbett's behalf, showed, as nothing else, the straits to which even the latter had been reduced. By the end of 1769 even the Garbetts were unable to meet the bills drawn on them.

A call of £500 on every £5,000 of stock held was not fruitful. So once again the banks were approached. In previous dealings the Company had limited itself to only one private and one chartered bank. With Gascoigne, this changed and he turned for help to a number of institutions, because the Company obviously stood a greater chance of borrowing a little from several than a substantial amount from one and also, as Adam Smith emphasised, because of the desirability of dealing with a number of banks, when circulating bills, so that the practice would be less easily detected. The Company's approaches were successful. Mansfield, Hunter and Company more than doubled their advance, from £7,000 to £15,000. The Thistle Bank offered £200 weekly to be settled by acceptance at four months, with the possibility of this being extended to six months, giving altogether £5,600. The British Linen Bank granted £100 weekly for 28 weeks, giving a total of £2,800. Then came an offer from a fateful source. The increased demand for credit in the developing Scottish economy led to the foundation in Ayr of Douglas, Heron and Company (the Ayr Bank) to try to remedy the apparent deficiency. Its policy was avowedly to make up for the inadequacies of the older banks in Edinburgh. On its first day of business the Ayr Bank wrote to Carron Company announcing that,

'having this day begun business here, and being fully satisfied of the utility of your Undertakings to this Country, which entitle you to every encouragement they can give; they have desired me to inform you that it was this day unanimously agreed to allow you a Cash Account of £5,000 stg. as a mark of their approbation and to desire that, if this is agreeable to you, and consistent with your present engagements, you would correspond with the Directors of the Edinburgh Branch, who are empowered to settle with you and whose business will begin in a few days.'

This offer was accepted with alacrity. This £5,000 was to be drawn at the rate of £300 a week and when this sum was exhausted it was agreed that the Company should continue to draw a weekly remittance from the bank of £300, but this was to be settled by acceptance payable at the bank's office at six month's date. This second line of credit provided another £8,400. Thus by the end of 1769 the Company was resting on a financial structure which provided a liberal and ready supply of funds with, however, the obvious disadvantage that, when the various credits were exhausted, large weekly commitments would fall due. These commitments would amount to £1,200 and £1,500 in alternate months from June to October 1770; thereafter they would amount to £2,400 and £3,000. Two sources were available to provide the means of meeting these liabilities as they became due. The first was the revenue from the Scottish sales, which it was not anticipated would be substantial until after September 1770. In any case much of this income was already earmarked to keep Mansfield, Hunter and Company's loan within reasonable proportions and to meet payments on Russian iron imported by the Company. The second source was the proceeds of the London sales held by Adam and Wiggins. Lest these should prove inadequate Gascoigne arranged, as a second line of defence, to meet any deficiency by drawing on a credit of £10,000 with the London bankers, Walpole, Clark and Bourne. However, the circulation of bills was still an easier solution. The increased help from the banks after 1769 did not end the practice, and when the acceptances for the banks fell due they were met, as were many other liabilities, by drawing bills on Mansfield, Hunter and Company, and more particularly on Adam and Wiggins, who in 1770 were given £6,000 by Carron Company to enable them to meet their engagements. From 1769 until the crisis of 1772 the Company was predominantly financed by the circulation of bills . . .

The precarious structure on which Carron Company rested in the early 1770's could continue only so long as those participating were themselves free from any financial debacles. The crisis of 1772 added further complications to the already precarious financial structure. The Ayr Bank and Francis Garbett and Company failed, while five of the individual partners of Carron Company, including Gascoigne, became bankrupt or suffered severe financial embarrassment. Though Samuel Garbett's official bankruptcy was postponed he never fully recovered from the effects of this crisis. In 1772 the Company was in an even more complicated financial tangle than in 1769. It is, in fact, surprising that it ever survived . . .

Against this sombre background Gascoigne had to conduct his

financial rescue operations. First, he faced the personal problems arising out of sequestration awarded against both Francis Garbett and Company and himself in the Court of Session in June 1772. Gascoigne countered this by presenting a cheerful picture of his own and the shipping company's affairs, had the sequestration held in suspense, and retained the management of his affairs in his own hands. The real state of Gascoigne's affairs was very different from the cheerful picture presented to his creditors. His shipping company was hopelessly in debt. Gascoigne had used the credit with Glyn and Halifax—guaranteed, of course, by Samuel Garbett—as a means of assisting some of the individual partners in Carron Company, particularly John Adam, whose family at that time was deeply involved in the Adelphi scheme in London. Garbett later alleged that Gascoigne circulated no less than £300,000 in bills for Adam, John Balfour (later a partner in the Company) and Balfour's partner, Gibson. Yet in the original presentation of his affairs to his creditors Gascoigne was not as culpable in his conduct as may be thought. As least part of the underestimate of his liabilities arose because he failed to take account of the bills in circulation, which, because of the inability of a large number of people to meet the demands made on them, eventually returned to be met by Francis Garbett and Company. Thus the first estimate of the debt of Francis Garbett and Company to Glyn and Halifax at the time of the bankruptcy was only £4,282, but when other returning bills were taken into account it became £50,300, while other claimants asked for about another £50,000. The debts of Francis Garbett and Company, particularly to Glyn and Halifax, Gascoigne hoped to foist on to Samuel Garbett. So he showed little interest in salvaging the shipping company, but, instead, turned his attention, almost wholly, to the more important Carron Company. Though the major blow to the Company had been the failure of the Ayr Bank and of some of the Company's individual partners, the failure of the shipping company also resulted in bills valued at about £9,600 returning on Carron Company because of non-payment. This might well have dealt it a fatal blow.

Gascoigne's first action after the crisis was to assure all and sundry that Carron Company had withstood it safely. Then he met the Company's initial difficulties quite simply by using his own resources, or more accurately, his creditors', to meet the bills as they returned on Carron from the bankrupt shipping company. In brief Gascoigne's creditors rescued the 'reeling' Carron Company in 1772, though unwittingly. This placed Gascoigne on the horns of a dilemma. Carron Company was unable to repay his advance at once, but Gascoigne's other assets were negligible. He had therefore to keep Carron Company solvent and, at the same time, prevent trouble among his own creditors by paying them a promised dividend at the beginning of 1774.

In such circumstances it is perhaps somewhat surprising that, except for a short period, the Company ceased circulating bills after the crisis of 1772. Yet the change is not unexpected. Confidence, of first importance for such circulation, had been severely shattered, and, in any case, the necessary links in Carron Company's system had been broken. The London end, Adam and Wiggins, had failed and in Scotland the Ayr Bank, which unlike others discounted bills freely, no longer functioned. Of necessity, the Company had to surrender the practice whether it wished to or not. The financing of the Company after the 1772 crisis was of a more stable and conventional nature. In particular, it was less expensive and less short-term. Again, however, the Company had to depend on the Scottish banks and their competitiveness. The Company's first bank, the Royal, had, of course, been displaced by the prodigally generous Ayr Bank. However, immediately after the crisis the Royal Bank agreed to discount weekly a bill for over £250 to be drawn by Gascoigne on the Company's law agent and to be repayable in three months. Later it granted more generous accommodation, discount of bills for £500 weekly payable after six months. In December 1772 more permanent accommodation was granted, an overdraft of £12,500, though on rather stiff terms, and only half of what was requested. The partners were disappointed and in 1773, in spite of many protestations of loyalty, Gascoigne scrapped the arrangements with the Royal Bank and approached the Bank of Scotland, which, again on proper security, loaned £7,500 to the Company and also paid off the Company's debt to the Royal Bank. One further transaction with banks, in 1774, completed Gascoigne's work in saving Carron Company. Mansfield, Hunter and Company, who, with only one other private bank in Edinburgh survived the 1772 crisis, offered to convert £10,000 of the balance due them by the Company through acceptances and on current account into a loan for a fixed period, if the Company provided heritable security. Through an extremely complicated transaction the Company advanced £3,000 and in return obtained two heritable bonds on a local estate, one for £3,000, the other for £9,000, which were immediately used to accept Mansfield, Hunter and Company's offer.

X

1 F. B. Hawley, *Enterprise and the Productive Process*, New York, 1907. pp. 113–26.

Enterprise stands on a different footing from, and above, the other productive factors. In the proper sense of the term, it alone is productive, the other three being simply forces set in motion, or released forces—the means by which it creates value. The question naturally arises as to whether they should not be considered conditions of, rather than factors in, the productive process. The answer seems to be that they should be treated wholly as means rather than causes were it not that an act of volition is always involved both in their creation and activity. While the enterpriser is the only direct creator of purchasing power, the landlord, capitalist and labourer are each voluntary creators of a condition essential to his activity . . .

While, therefore, land, capital and labour stand on a different footing from enterprise, they are . . . correctly considered to be subsidiary productive factors . . .

Historically considered, the influence which, more than any other, debarred the economist from an appreciation of the peculiar theoretic position of the Enterpriser, or as he was then called, the Entrepreneur, was the almost unquestioned supremacy during so many years of the dogma of 'laissez faire', founded upon the assumption that each producer, being the best judge of how the productive factor or factors he controlled could be most advantageously utilised for himself, would necessarily, if left to his own initiative, in benefiting himself accomplish also what was best for the community . . . the understanding of Enterprise we have now reached unveils, however, the falsity of the assumption on which the economic dogma of 'laissez faire' is based, namely, that the controller of the three subsidiary productive factors have as much voice as enterprise in the direction of production, whereas the truth is that they have no influence at all upon it as producers, but only an indirect influence as consumers. Subject to the limitation that he must produce what consumers will pay him for at a renumeration rate, the enterpriser is the sole arbiter as to the method and direction of production . . . The direction of production—what shall be produced, how much of it, and by what method—lies wholly with the enterpriser, who will allow the landlords, the capitalists, and the labourers only what prevailing conditions enforce.

---

2 L. M. Fraser, *Economic Thought and Language*, London, 1937. pp. 318–20.

What, then, is the factor of production enterprise? In ordinary language the word has two main meanings. In the first instance it refers to a thing projected or attempted—particularly if it be of a bold or hazardous nature. But it may also be used subjectively of the quality or qualities possessed by those who undertake such projects—that is to say, it may be in effect a synonym for "boldness" or "initiative". Both these meanings are to be found in economic writings: but in addition the word has come to be used in at least two rather more specialised ways. On the one hand it has become more concrete, standing for the *result* or objective realisation of a project in the economic field—viz. a firm or business unit. And on the other hand it has become more abstract, being used of the *activities involved* in initiating or running such a project . . .

Now it is in the fourth sense of the word that enterprise is to be thought of as a factor of production. It is an activity on the part of the entrepreneur—a contribution which he makes to the creation of wealth. And our next task must be to find out who the entrepreneur is and what precise form his productive activities take.

Superficially, at least, there is a wide measure of agreement on this point. Almost every economist would be prepared to accept the following propositions, though there might be some dispute as to their relative importance for the theory of value.

(1) The entrepreneur is responsible for the control or direction of a firm or company. It is on his initiative that it is brought into existence. Moreover, when it is a going concern he decides what its policy shall be—what alterations shall be made in its internal structure, in the volume of its output, and in the prices it offers to owners of productive resources or demands from consumers; what advantages can be taken of current technical progress; whether general conditions justify an extension of its plant or call for retrenchment; and so on. On the other hand, he is *not* concerned, qua entrepreneur, with the day to day supervision of the productive process itself. Enterprise is connected, in short, with "innovation" and "adjustment"; but not with industrial management in the narrower sense.

(2) Upon the entrepreneur falls the brunt of any risk or uncertainty which the initiating and running of the concern may involve. If it is successful he claims the profits; if it is unsuccessful he must bear the loss.

(3) So far as the market is concerned the entrepreneur is a middleman. He buys productive resources from their owners—labourers, landlords, etc.—and sells the product they yield to the consumers. He is in fact the intermediary between production and consumption, between the factor markets and the commodity markets; and on his decisions depend the distribution of the community's resources among the various uses to which they may be put.

XI

The Law Book of the Crowley Ironworks, ed. M. W. Flinn in *Publications of the Surtees Society*, CLXVII, Durham, 1957. pp. 60–2.

Order Number 85

EXTRAVAGANCIES DISCOURAGED

Whereas William Sparling by lawsuits and contentions, Benjamin Lee and Richard Collins by whoreing, Humphrey Vincent by pride and high eating, Thomas Holland and Simon Yarrow by pride, Saml. Barker by gameing, and Wm. Inning by sotting, and John Halford by trading, have all rendered themselves unfitt for any business, and reduced themselves into extreme poverty, and to a great degree fall short in the dischargeing themselves. And such has been the combination and confederacie of sundry of these villans to associate themselves together, thinking if they can but keep each other's evil actions from me, they are in safety; and have by their said bad practices kept their evil actions so long from us that it hath been too late to remedy the same, and they left in a most miserable and deplorable condition. And as a master I am bound in conscience to do my best to prevent these dangerous consequences in servants, and as a father to take care that my estate is not wasted by the extravagancies of such villains.

1. For remedy I do order and require the Treasurer to make it his business to pry and enquire into the actions of all clerks whatever, and if he findeth any guilty of the said vices, or have broke or acted contrary to any order whatever, to inform me.

2. That if any clerk whatever under me shall be guilty of any extravagancies that shall or may lead them to spend more than their wages allowed, then to inform me.

3. That if in case any of my clerks that are married or apprentices shall keep any woman's company (although they have as much sanctity as John Halford and Mr. Inning), the Treasurer is to fully inform me.

4. In case any of my clerks (other than married) or apprentices shall keep any woman company that have been reputed whores or are under a light character, the Treasurer is to inform me.

5. In case any of my clerks or servants whatever shall any ways lay out or spend more than their salaries, let their pretences be what it will, be sure to inform me.

6. When any clerk or servant shall make a frequent practice in going much abroad, particularly to Newcastle which hath been the ruine of several, to inform me.

7. In case the Treasurer shall through friendship, or for want of informing himself, or by connivance conceal any of the vices of any of my clerks, I will resent it so as to discharge him.

8. Whereas Mr. Crowley hath made it his observation that morning drinking hath been of fatal consequence to all that have made a practice of it: 1. It is of all things the most destructive to business, 2. It destroyeth health, memory and understanding, 3. It produceth nothing but folly and madness, 4. It wastes the only time to do business; all of which Mr. Crowley hath taken into consideration in a most serious manner and hath totally broke it at London even to go and drink in a morning with customers and hath found the same to be obligeing and not offensive to the best of customers; it is therefore declared that Mr. Crowley will take effectual care to discharge all such as shall for the future practice the drinking of any strong liquor before they go to dinner. And to the end such persons may be discovered, the Treasurer is hereby obliged in every State of Cash the Unit shall be 6, to mention every clerk's name in particular and to say 'Except those which I have fixed and have set a ◊ against, I have not heard of their drinking on mornings and I believe they have no ways practiced drinking strong liquors in a morning'.

XII

Robert Owen, *A New View of Society*, 1813, Pelican Classic Edition, 1969, pp. 114–20.

In the year 1784 the late Mr Dale of Glasgow founded a manufactory for spinning of cotton near the falls of the Clyde, in the county of Lanark in Scotland; and about that period cotton mills were first introduced into the northern part of the kingdom.

It was the power which could be obtained from the falls of water which induced Mr Dale to erect his mills in this situation, for in other respects it was not well chosen; the country around was uncultivated; the inhabitants were poor, and few in number; and the roads in the neighbourhood were so bad, that the Falls now so celebrated were then unknown to strangers.

It was therefore necessary to collect a new population to supply the infant establishment with labourers. This however was no light task; for all the regularly trained Scotch peasantry disdained the idea of working early and late, day after day, within cotton mills. Two modes then only remained of obtaining these labourers; the one, to procure children from the various public charities of the country; and the other, to induce families to settle around the works.

To accommodate the first, a large house was erected, which ultimately contained about five hundred children, who were procured chiefly from the workhouses and charities in Edinburgh. These children were to be fed, clothed, and educated; and these duties Mr Dale performed with the unwearied benevolence which it is well known he possessed.

To obtain the second, a village was built, and the houses were let at a low rent to such families as could be induced to accept employment in the mills: but such was the general dislike to that occupation at the time, that, with a few exceptions, only persons destitute of friends, employment, and character, were found willing to try the experiment; and of these a sufficient number to supply a constant increase of the manufactory could not be obtained. It was therefore deemed a favour on the part even of such individuals to reside at the village, and when taught the business they grew so valuable to the establishment, that they became agents not to be governed contrary to their own inclinations.

Mr Dale's principal advocations were at a distance from the works, which he seldom visited more than once for a few hours in three or four months: he was therefore under the necessity of committing the management of the establishment to various servants with more or less power.

Those who have a practical knowledge of mankind will readily anticipate the character which a population so collected and constituted would acquire; it is therefore scarcely necessary to state, that the community by degrees was formed under these circumstances into a very wretched society; every man did that which was right in his own eyes, and vice and immorality prevailed to a monstrous extent. The population lived in idleness, in poverty, in almost every kind of crime; consequently in debt, out of health, and in misery. Yet to make matters still worse,— although the cause proceeded from the best possible motive, a conscientious adherence to principle,—the whole was under a strong sectarian influence, which gave a marked and decided preference to one set of religious opinions over all others, and the professors of the favoured opinions were the privileged of the community.

The boarding-house containing the children presented a very different scene. The benevolent proprietor spared no expense to give comfort to the poor children. The rooms provided for them were spacious, always clean, and well ventilated; the food was abundant, and of the best quality; the clothes were neat and useful; a surgeon was kept in constant pay to direct how to prevent or to cure disease; and the best instructors which the country afforded were appointed to teach such branches of education as were deemed likely to be useful to children in their situation. Kind and well disposed persons were appointed to superintend all their proceedings. Nothing, in short, at first sight seemed wanting to render it a most complete charity.

But to defray the expense of these well devised arrangements, and support the establishment generally, it was absolutely necessary that the children should be employed within the mills from six o'clock in the morning till seven in the evening, summer and winter; and after these hours their education commenced. The directors of the public charities, from mistaken economy, would not consent to send the children under their care to cotton mills, unless the children were received by the proprietors at the ages of six, seven, and eight. And Mr Dale was under the necessity of accepting them at those ages, or of stopping the manufactory which he had commenced.

It is not to be supposed that children so young could remain, with the interval of meals only, from six in the morning until seven in the evening, in constant employment on their feet within cotton mills, and afterwards acquire much proficiency in education. And so it proved; for many of them became dwarfs in body and mind, and some of them were deformed. Their labour through the day, and their education at night, became so irksome, that numbers of them continually ran away, and almost all looked forward with impatience and anxiety to the expiration of their apprenticeship of seven, eight and nine years; which generally expired when they were from thirteen to fifteen years old. At this period of life, unaccustomed to provide for themselves, and unacquainted with the world, they usually went to Edinburgh or Glasgow, where boys and girls were soon assailed by the innumerable temptations which all large towns present; and to which many of them fell sacrifices.

Thus Mr Dale's arrangements and kind solicitude for the comfort and happiness of these children were rendered in their ultimate effect almost nugatory. They were hired by him, and sent to be employed, and without their labour he could not support them; but, while under his care, he did all that any individual, circumstanced as he was, could do for his fellow-creatures. The error proceeded from the children being sent from the workhouses at an age much too young for employment; they ought to have been detained four years longer, and educated; and then some of the evils which followed would have been prevented.

If such a true picture, not overcharged, of parish apprentices to our manufacturing system, under the best and most humane regulations, in what colours must it be exhibited under the worst?

Mr Dale was advancing in years; he had no son to succeed him; and finding the consequences just described to be the result of all his strenuous exertions for the improvement and happiness of his fellow-creatures, it is not surprising that he became disposed to retire from the cares of the establishment. He accordingly sold it to some English merchants and manufacturers; one of whom, under the circumstances just narrated, undertook the management of the concern, and fixed his residence in the midst of the population. This individual had been previously in the management of large establishments, employing a number of work-people in the neighbourhood of Manchester; and in every case, by the steady application of certain general principles, he succeeded in reforming the habits of those under his care, and who always among their associates in similar employment appeared conspicuous for their good conduct. With this previous succeess in remodelling English character, but ignorant of the local ideas, manners, and customs of those now committed to his management, the stranger commenced his task.

At that period the lower classes in Scotland, like those of other countries, had strong prejudices against strangers having any authority over them, and particularly against the English; few of whom had then settled in Scotland, and not one in the neighbourhood of the scenes under description. It is also well known that even the Scotch peasantry and working classes possess the habit of making observations and reasoning thereon with great acuteness; and in the present case, those employed naturally concluded that the new purchasers intended merely to make the utmost profit by the establishment, from the abuses of which many of themselves were then deriving support. The persons employed at these works were therefore strongly prejudiced against the new director of the establishment; prejudiced because he was a stranger and from England; because he succeeded Mr Dale, under whose proprietorship they acted almost as they liked; because his religious creed was not theirs; and because they concluded that the works would be governed by new laws and regulations, calculated to squeeze, as they often termed it, the greatest sum of gain out of their labour.

In consequence, from the day he arrived among them, every means which ingenuity could devise was set to work to counteract the plan which he attempted to introduce; and for two years it was a regular attack and defence of prejudices and malpractices between the manager and population of the place; without the former being able to make such progress, or convince the latter of the sincerity of his good intentions for their welfare. He however did not lose his patience, his temper, or his confidence in the certain success of the principles on which he founded his conduct. These principles ultimately prevailed: the population could not continue to resist a firm well-directed kindness administering justice to all. They therefore slowly and cautiously began to give him some portion of their confidence; and, as this increased, he was enabled more and more to develop his plans for their amelioration. It may with truth be said, that at this period they possessed almost all the vices and very few of the virtues of a social community. Theft and the receipt of stolen goods was their trade, idleness and drunkenness their habit, falsehood and deception their garb, dissentions civil and religious their daily practice: they united only in a zealous systematic opposition to their employers.

Here, then, was a fair field on which to try the efficacy in practice of principles supposed capable of altering any characters. The manager formed his plans accordingly: he spent some time in finding out the full extent of the evil against which he had to contend, and in tracing the true causes which had produced, and were continuing, those effects. He found that all was distrust, disorder, and disunion; and he wished to introduce confidence, regularity, and harmony: he therefore began to bring forward his various expedients to withdraw the unfavourable circumstances by which they had been hitherto surrounded, and replace them by others calculated to produce a more happy result.

XIII

Henry Ford, *My Life and Work*, 1922. pp. 67–75.

From the day the first motor car appeared on the streets it had to me appeared to be a necessity. It was this knowledge and assurance that led me to build to the one end—a car that would meet the wants of the multitudes. All my efforts were then and still are turned to the production of one car—one model. And, year following year, the pressure was, and still is, to improve and refine and make better, with an increasing reduction in price. The universal car had to have these attributes:

(1) Quality in material to give service in use. Vanadium steel is the strongest, toughest, and most lasting of steels. It forms the foundation and super-structure of the cars. It is the highest quality steel in this respect in the world, regardless of price.

(2) Simplicity in operation—because the masses are not mechanics.

(3) Power in sufficient quantity.

(4) Absolute reliability—because of the varied uses to which the cars would be put and the variety of roads over which they would travel.

(5) Lightness. With the Ford there are only 7·95 points to be carried by each cubic inch of piston displacement. This is one of the reasons why Ford cars are "always going", wherever and whenever you see them—through sand and mud, through slush, snow, and water, up hills, across fields and roadless plains.

(6) Control—to hold its speed always in hand, calmly and safely meeting every emergency and contingency either in the crowded

streets of the city or on dangerous roads. The planetary transmission of the Ford gave this control and anybody could work it. That is the "why" of the saying: "Anybody can drive a Ford". It can turn around almost anywhere.

(7) The more a motor car weighs, naturally the more fuel and lubricants are used in the driving; the lighter the weight, the lighter the expense of operation. The light weight of the Ford car in its early years was used as an argument against it. Now that is all changed.

The design which I settled upon was called "Model T". The important feature of the new model—which, if it were accepted, as I thought it would be, I intended to make the only model and then start into real production—was its simplicity. There were but four constructional units in the car—the power plant, the frame, the front axle, and the rear axle. All of these were easily accessible and they were designed so that no special skill would be required for their repair or replacement. I believed then, although I said very little about it because of the novelty of the idea, that it ought to be possible to have parts so simple and so inexpensive that the menace of expensive hand repair work would be entirely eliminated. The parts could be made so cheaply that it would be less expensive to buy new ones than to have old ones repaired. They could be carried in hardware shops just as nails or bolts are carried. I thought that it was up to me as the designer to make the car so completely simple that no one could fail to understand it.

That works both ways and applies to everything. The less complex an article, the easier it is to make, the cheaper it may be sold, and therefore the greater number may be sold.

It is not necessary to go into the technical details of the construction but perhaps this is as good a place as any to review the various models, because "Model T" was the last of the models and the policy which it brought about took this business out of the ordinary line of business. Application of the same idea would take any business out of the ordinary run . . .

The "Model T" had practically no features which were not contained in some one or other of the previous models. Every detail had been fully tested in practice. There was no guessing as to whether or not it would be a successful model. It had to be. There was no way it could escape being so, for it had not been made in a day. It contained all that I was then able to put into a motor car plus the material, which for the first time I was able to obtain. We put out "Model T" for the season 1908–1909.

The company was then five years old. The original factory space had been ·28 acre. We had employed an average of 311 people in the first year, built 1,708 cars, and had one branch house. In 1908, the factory space had increased to 2·65 acres and we owned the building. The average number of employees had increased to 1,908. We built 6,181 cars and had fourteen branch houses. It was a prosperous business.

During the season 1908–1909 we continued to make Models "R" and "S", four-cylinder runabouts and roadsters, the models that had previously been so successful, and which sold at $700 and $750. But "Model T" swept them right out. We sold 10,607 cars—a larger number than any manufacturer had ever sold. The price for the touring car was $850. On the same chassis we mounted a town car at $1,000, a roadster at $825, a coupe at $950, and a landaulet at $950.

This season demonstrated conclusively to me that it was time to put the new policy in force. The salesmen, before I had announced the policy, were spurred by the great sales to think that even greater sales might be had if only we had more models. It is strange how, just as soon as an article becomes successful, somebody starts to think that it would be more successful if only it were different. There is a tendency to keep monkeying with styles and to spoil a good thing by changing it. The salesmen were insistent on increasing the line. They listened to the 5 per cent., the special customers who could say what they wanted, and forgot all about the 95 per cent. who just bought without making any fuss. No business can improve unless it pays the closest possible attention to complaints and suggestions. If there is any defect in service then that must be instantly and rigorously investigated, but when the suggestion is only as to style, one has to make sure whether it is not merely a personal whim that is being voiced. Salesmen always want to cater to whims instead of acquiring sufficient knowledge of their product to be able to explain to the customer with the whim that what they have will satisfy his every requirement—that is, of course, provided what they have does satisfy these requirements.

Therefore in 1909 I announced one morning, without any previous warning, that in the future we were going to build only one model, that the model was going to be "Model T", and that the chassis would be exactly the same for all cars, and I remarked:

> "Any customer can have a car painted any colour that he wants so long as it is black."

I cannot say that any one agreed with me. The selling people could not of course see the advantages that a single model would bring about in production. More than that, they did not particularly care. They thought that our production was good enough as it was and there was a very decided opinion that lowering the sales price would hurt sales, that the people who wanted quality would be driven away and that there would be none to replace them. There was very little conception of the motor industry. A motor car was still regarded as something in the way of a luxury. The manufacturers did a good deal to spread this idea. Some clever persons invented the name "pleasure car" and the advertising emphasized the pleasure features. The sales people had ground for their objections and particularly when I made the following announcement:

> I will build a motor car for the great multitude. It will be large enough for the family but small enough for the individual to run and care for. It will be constructed of the best materials, by the best men to be hired, after the simplest designs that modern engineering can devise. But it will be so low in price that no man making a good salary will be unable to own one—and enjoy with his family the blessing of hours of pleasure in God's great open spaces.

This announcement was received not without pleasure. The general comment was:

> "If Ford does that he will be out of business in six months."

The impression was that a good car could not be built at a low price, and that, anyhow, there was no use in building a low-priced car because only wealthy people were in the market for cars. The

1908–1909 sales of more than ten thousand cars had convinced me that we needed a new factory. We already had a big modern factory—the Piquette Street plant. It was as good as, perhaps a little better than, any automobile factory in the country. But I did not see how it was going to care for the sales and production that were inevitable. So I bought sixty acres at Highland Park, which was then considered away out in the country from Detroit. The amount of ground bought and the plans for a bigger factory than the world has ever seen were opposed. The question was already being asked:

"How soon will Ford blow up?"

Nobody knows how many thousand times it has been asked since. It is asked only because of the failure to grasp that a principle rather than an individual is at work, and the principle is so simple that it seems mysterious.

For 1909–1910, in order to pay for the new land and buildings, I slightly raised the prices. This is perfectly justifiable and results in a benefit, not an injury, to the purchaser. I did exactly the same thing a few years ago—or rather, in that case I did not lower the price as is my annual custom, in order to build the River Rouge plant. The extra money might in each case have been had by borrowing, but then we should have had a continuing charge upon the business and all subsequent cars would have had to bear this charge. The price of all the models was increased $100, with the exception of the roadster, which was increased only $75 and of the landaulet and two car, which were increased $150 and $200 respectively. We sold 18,664 cars, and then for 1910–1911, with the new facilities, I cut the touring car from $950 to $780 and we sold 34,528 cars. That is the beginning of the steady reduction in the price of the cars in the face of ever-increasing cost of materials and ever-higher wages.

Contrast the year 1908 with the year 1911. The factory space increased from 2·65 to 32 acres. The average number of employees from 1,908 to 4,110, and the cars built from a little over six thousand to nearly thirty-five thousand. You will note that men were not employed in proportion to the output.

We were, almost overnight it seems, in great production. How did all this come about?

Simply through the application of an inevitable principle. By the application of intelligently directed power and machinery. In a little dark shop on a side street an old man had laboured for years making axe handles. Out of seasoned hickory he fashioned them, with the help of a draw shave, a chisel, and a supply of sandpaper. Carefully was each handle weighed and balanced. Not two of them were alike. The curve must exactly fit the hand and must conform to the grain of the wood. From dawn until dark the old man laboured. His average product was eight handles a week, for which he received a dollar and a half each. And often some of these were unsaleable—because the balance was not true.

To-day you can buy a better axe handle, made by machinery, for a few cents. And you need not worry about the balance. They are all alike—and every one is perfect. Modern methods applied in a big way have not only brought the cost of axe handles down to a fraction of their former cost—but they have immensely improved the product.

It was the application of these same methods to the making of the Ford car that at the very start lowered the price and heightened the quality. We just developed an idea.

XIV

Sir Thomas J. Lipton, *Leaves from the Lipton Logs*, 1931. pp. 95–102.

The trouble in the 'seventies was that few people could be induced to take advertising seriously. It has frequently been said that I was one of the earliest pioneers in the movement which brought about the stupendous change whereby advertising now ranks as one of the most highly-specialized and essential branches of British and American business. And however that may be, it is certainly true that I was one of the first Britishers to see the immense possibilities and advantages to be reaped from novel and judicious advertising.

Even in these early days I found myself toying with the idea of advertising my shop and its wares. I have told you that of the original hundred pounds capital, I only used about half in starting the shop, the rest remaining on deposit receipt at the bank until such time as I could hit upon some suitable method of employing it. Well, after much serious thought I determined to use a portion of the money in advertising. During my travels in America I had observed that the firms that were making good were all regular advertisers. One couplet I remembered having seen in New York was to the effect that:

> "The man who on his trade relies
> Must either bust or advertise."

And these two simple but effective lines kept constantly recurring to my mind.

My first essay in the art of advertising was a very simple handbill urging all housewives who wanted superb value at the lowest possible prices to patronize Lipton's Market in Stobcross Street. Later I posted a circular containing my prices—and asking for a comparison with those of other traders—to a few hundred specially selected addresses in my vicinity. Then I tried a small "ad" in a Glasgow evening newspaper, drawing attention to a line of extra fine bacon to be had at my shop at a price which "defied competition". This advertisement cost me seven shillings and sixpence—the forerunner of many hundreds of thousands of pounds spent by the Lipton firm in the newspaper press of the old and new worlds.

But how to discover something really novel in the shape of an advertisement without expending much money? This was my next problem. Handbills, smartly-worded window cards, newspaper "inches" or larger spaces were all very well so far as they went, but I was not satisfied that these efforts were sufficient. If I could invent something that would make people talk, or, better still, make them laugh, I would, it seemed to my mind, be much nearer solving the problem of effective advertising. In the opening weeks of my trading I had noticed that a smile and a joke were generally well received by my customers, and I also noted this human characteristic—that people in a good humour will always spend more freely than those with a frown on their face. Therefore, I kept telling myself, the best ideas behind successful advertising must be those with a smile in them. But it was difficult to hit upon just the right notion to begin with; once started, I knew very well that other suggestions would follow automatically.

Suddenly one morning the bright idea struck me that it might be a good thing to have a large wooden ham, painted as realistically as possible, hung from a pole outside the shop door. Nobody passing up or down the street could miss the sign and insignia of the shop's principal contents. I had the idea carried out forthwith. The swinging ham attracted quite a lot of attention immediately. Indeed, it was far more successful than I had imagined, for it was put up on a very hot day, the sun promptly melted the paint on the ham, and, lo and behold! the latter became an almost perfect example of a large, luscious ham straight from the boiling! It caused endless amusement among the passers-by and soon people came from all over the district to see "Lipton's greasy ham"!

From a single ham to an entire pig was, obviously, an easy step. In fact, two pigs—the largest, fattest, finest porkers I could buy at the Glasgow live-stock market! These I had removed to a private yard and scrubbed and polished until they looked the most respectable pair of hogs ever seen out of Smithfield Show. I put pink and blue ribbons round their necks and tassels on their tails to match, and had them driven through the streets with a large banner suspended over them and bearing the words "Lipton's Orphans". Long before they had arrived opposite the shop in Stobcross Street the pigs had collected a vast crowd. The scheme had been a triumphant success. Everybody asked every other body what the joke was, who the pigs belonged to, and the entire crowd was kept in constant merriment by the antics of the pigs all along the "line of march".

This new method of driving the traditional pigs "to market" was too good to drop. I employed the same pigs over and over again, but always took care to see that they followed a different route to Stobcross Street. A variation of the "stunt" was to have a typical Irishman, knee-breeches, cutaway coat, billycock hat, shillelagh an' all an' all, "steering" an enormous porker through the most crowded thoroughfares of the city. On the pig's sides were painted the words: "I'm going to Lipton's. The best shop in town for Irish Bacon!"

As often as not the Lipton pigs, being the largest and fattest I could find, took it into their heads to lie down in the middle of the street and refuse to budge an inch. At Glasgow Cross on one occasion a "procession" of "Lipton's Orphans" all decided to have a siesta together on the tram-lines, and traffic was entirely suspended for quite a long time.

There are many people still alive in Glasgow who will tell you that these orphan-pigs laid the foundation of my fortunes. In any case I cannot deny that my idea of advertising by means of live pigs created a first-class sensation all over the city. The novelty of the whole thing appealed to people and made them laugh. My name was on everybody's lips. And that was all I wanted. Customers came to the shop in ever-increasing numbers, and in less than six months after I had taken down the shutters for the first time I had to extend my premises.

My next novelty in advertising was to secure the whole-time services of Willie Lockhart, one of the finest cartoonists in Scotland. Willie was a good-natured fellow, but a Bohemian with an artistic temperament who knew nothing of business. The fact that he, of all people, should now join my staff looked like sheer madness to old trade-rivals, and they made it the target for many a joke. "What in the wide world had cartoons to do with selling eggs and bacon ?" they asked. They had not to wait long to see.

The first cartoon Lockhart drew for me reduced to paper the same idea of "Lipton's Orphans" as had been used a few days before in the street-processions. It took the form of a large humorous poster which, prominently displayed in the window, drew crowds to the shop. The scene depicted in the cartoon was that of a solitary pig, its eyes streaming with tears, perched on the back of an Irish drover, while near by stood an old lady, full of concern for the animal's grief. And underneath was this letter-press:

OLD LADY: "Why, my good man, what ails your pig ?"
THE IRISHMAN: "Sure ma'am, he's an orphan; the rest of the family have gone to Lipton's."

This simple cartoon drew thousands of people to my window, and regularly, thereafter, a fresh cartoon was pasted up every Monday morning. People came from all over the town to look at them, and they always went away with a smile on their faces. One very successful cartoon, I remember, was inspired by the fall of one of the Gladstone Ministries. One half of the picture was devoted to the defeated Cabinet in terribly woe-begone plight, while the other half showed the same statesmen, headed by the Illustrious William Ewart Gladstone himself, emerging joyfully from my shop and each brandishing a sturdy ham by its shank. The smile on Mr. Gladstone's face as he gazed aloft at his particular ham made all Glasgow laugh uproariously. I never saw such a comic laugh on any human face; I chuckled myself every time I looked at the cartoon.

The idea behind the cartoon was, of course, that so long as Lipton's Market was to the fore, there was no excuse for prolonged despondency anywhere—not even in a defeated British Cabinet!

Lockhart's drawings were so successful that I put him on to do pictorial price-cards for the goods in the windows. Some of these were most amusing, particularly one entitled: "Great Fall in

Eggs". This showed a fat policeman who, foiled in an effort to climb a wall over which a burglar was escaping, had fallen slap into a crate of eggs. It was rumoured that Willie Lockhart had taken for his model a certain Glasgow policeman against whom he had a grudge. Be this as it may, I know that every policeman in the city came to have a look at the picture, and many of them became customers at my shop.

Nor was it solely in cartoons and pictures that Lockhart's gifts found their full artistic scope, for under my guidance and encouragement he blossomed forth into a sculptor on highly original lines. The Lipton "statuary in butter" was soon known far and wide. Lockhart could convert a firkin of butter into a dozen different and pleasing designs; perhaps his greatest triumph in this line being a tableau representing a stout policeman making love to a pretty dairymaid. Lockhart's policemen and all his other male characters—whether drawn by pencil or brush, or built up of butter, cheese—sausages, even—were, without exception, happy-featured, heavy-paunched, and jovial to the last degree. Neither he nor I had any use whatever for skinny, miserable types; these were entirely foreign to our ideas and to the wares sold by Thomas Lipton!

XV

J. S. Mill, *Principles of Political Economy*, 1848, ed. W. Ashley, 1909. pp. 101–15.

We have concluded our general survey of the requisites of production. We have found that they may be reduced to three: labour, capital, and the materials and motive forces afforded by nature . . .

We now advance to the second great question in political economy; on what the degree of productiveness of these agents depends. For it is evident that their productive efficacy varies greatly at various times and places. With the same population and extent of territory, some countries have a much larger amount of production than others, and the same country at one time a greater amount than itself at another. Compare England either with a similar extent of territory in Russia, or with an equal population of Russians. Compare England now with England in the Middle Ages; Sicily, Northern Africa, or Syria at present, with the same countries at the time of their greatest prosperity, before the Roman Conquest. Some of the causes which contribute to this difference of productiveness are obvious; others not so much so. We proceed to specify several of them.

The most evident cause of superior productiveness is what are called natural advantages. These are various. Fertility of soil is one of the principal . . .

A favourable climate is even more important than a rich soil . . .

Among natural advantages, besides soil and climate, must be mentioned abundance of mineral productions, in convenient situations, and capable of being worked with moderate labour . . . But perhaps a greater advantage than all these is a maritime situation, especially when accompanied with good natural harbours; and, next to it, great navigable rivers. These advantages consist indeed wholly in saving of cost of carriage. But few who have not considered the subject, have any adequate notion how great an extent of economical advantage this comprises; nor, without having considered the influence exercised on production by exchanges, and by what is called the division of labour, can it be fully estimated. So important is it, that it often does more than counterbalance sterility of soil, and almost every other natural inferiority; especially in that early stage of industry in which labour and science have not yet provided artificial means of communication capable of rivalling the natural . . .

So much for natural advantages; the value of which, *caeteris paribus*, is too obvious to be ever underrated. But experience testifies that natural advantages scarcely ever do for a community, no more than fortune and station do for an individual, anything like what it lies in their nature, or in their capacity, to do. Neither now nor in former ages have the nations possessing the best climate and soil been either the richest or the most powerful; but (in so far as regards the mass of the people) generally among the poorest, though, in the midst of poverty, probably on the whole the most enjoying. Human life in those countries can be supported on so little, that the poor seldom suffer from anxiety, and in climates in which mere existence is a pleasure, the luxury which they prefer is that of repose. Energy, at the call of passion, they possess in abundance, but not that which is manifested in sustained and persevering labour: and as they seldom concern themselves enough about remote objects to establish good political institutions, the incentives to industry are further weakened by imperfect protection of its fruits. Successful production, like most other kinds of success, depends more on the qualities of the human agents, than on the circumstances in which they work: and it is difficulties, not facilities, that nourish bodily and mental energy. Accordingly the tribes of mankind who have overrun and conquered others, and compelled them to labour for their benefit, have been mostly reared amidst hardship . . .

As the second, therefore, of the causes of superior productiveness, we may rank the greater energy of labour. By this is not to be understood occasional, but regular and habitual energy . . . Individuals, or nations, do not differ so much in the efforts they are able and willing to make under strong immediate incentives, as in their capacity of present exertion for a distant object; and in the thoroughness of their application to work on ordinary occasions. Some amount of these qualities is a necessary condition of any great improvement among mankind . . .

The third element which determines the productiveness of the labour of a community, is the skill and knowledge therein existing; whether it be the skill and knowledge of the labourers themselves, or of those who direct their labour. No illustration is requisite to show how the efficacy of industry is promoted by the manual dexterity of those who perform mere routine processes; by the intelligence of those engaged in operations in which the mind has a considerable part; and by the amount of knowledge of natural powers and of the properties of objects, which is turned to the purposes of industry. That the productiveness of the labour of a people is limited by their knowledge of the arts of life, is self-evident; and that any progress in those arts, any improved application of the objects or powers of nature to industrial uses, enables the same quantity and intensity of labour to raise a greater produce.

One principal department of these improvements consists in the invention and use of tools and machinery . . .

But the effects of the increased knowledge of a community in increasing its wealth, need the less illustration as they have become familiar to the most uneducated, from such conspicuous instances as railways and steam-ships. A thing not yet so well understood and recognised, is the economical value of the general diffusion of intelligence among the people. The number of persons fitted to direct and superintend any industrial enterprise, or even to execute any process which cannot be reduced almost to an affair of memory and routine, is always far short of the demand; as is evident from the enormous difference between the salaries paid to such persons and the wages of ordinary labour. The deficiency of practical good sense, which renders the majority of the labouring class such bad calculators—which makes, for instance, their domestic economy so improvident, lax, and irregular—must disqualify them for any but a low grade of intelligent labour, and render their industry far less productive than with equal energy it otherwise might be. The importance, even in this limited aspect, of popular education, is well worthy of the attention of politicians, especially in England; since competent observers, accustomed to employ labourers of various nations, testify that in the workman of other countries they often find great intelligence wholly apart from instruction, but that if an English labourer is anything but a hewer of wood and a drawer of water, he is indebted for it to education, which in his case is almost always self-education . . .

The moral qualities of the labourers are fully as important to the efficiency and worth of their labour, as the intellectual. Independently of the effects of intemperance upon their bodily and mental faculties, and of flighty, unsteady habits upon the energy and continuity of their work (points so easily understood as not to require being insisted upon), it is well worthy of meditation, how much of the aggregate effect of their labour depends on their trustworthiness. All the labour now expended in watching that they fulfil their engagement, or in verifying that they have fulfilled it, is so much withdrawn from the real business of production, to be devoted to a subsidiary function rendered needful not by the necessity of things, but by the dishonesty of men. Nor are the greatest outward precautions more than very imperfectly effiicacious, where, as is now almost invariably the case with hired labourers, the slightest relaxation of vigilance is an opportunity eagerly seized for eluding performance of their contract. The advantage to mankind of being able to trust one another, penetrates into every crevice and cranny of human life: the economical is perhaps the smallest part of it, yet even this is incalculable . . .

Among the secondary causes which determine the productiveness of productive agents, the most important is Security. By security I mean the completeness of the protection which society affords to its members. This consists of protection *by* the government, and protection *against* the government. The latter is the more important. Where a person known to possess anything worth taking away, can expect nothing but to have it torn from him, with every circumstance of tyrannical violence, by the agents of a rapacious government, it is not likely that many will exert themselves to produce much more than necessaries . . .

Much of the security of person and property in modern nations is the effect of manners and opinion rather than of law . . .

Independently of all imperfection in the bulwarks which society purposely throws round what it recognises as property, there are various other modes in which defective institutions impede the employment of the productive resources of a country to the best advantage. We shall have occasion for noticing many of these in the progress of our subject. It is sufficient here to remark, that the efficiency of industry may be expected to be great, in proportion as the fruits of industry are insured to the person exerting it: and that all social arrangements are conducive to useful exertion, according as they provide that the reward of every one for his labour shall be proportioned as much as possible to the benefit which it produces. All laws or usages which favour one class or sort of persons to the disadvantage of others; which chain up the efforts of any part of the community in pursuit of their own good, or stand between those efforts and their natural fruits—are (independently of all other grounds of condemnation) violations of the fundamental principles of economical policy; tending to make the aggregate productive powers of the community productive in a less degree than they would otherwise be.

XVI

John Calvin, *Institutes of the Christian Religion*, 1536, Book III, Chapter VII, paragraphs 8 and 9. Translation H. Y. Beveridge, London, 1953.

We have a frenzied desire, an infinite eagerness, to pursue wealth and honour, intrigue for power, accumulate riches, and collect all those frivolities which seem conducive to luxury and splendour. On the other hand, we have a remarkable dread, a remarkable hatred of poverty, mean birth, and a humble condition, and feel the strongest desire to guard against them. Hence, in regard to those who frame their life after their own counsel, we see how restless they are in mind, how many plans they try, to what fatigues they submit, in order that they may gain what avarice or ambition desires, or, on the other hand, escape poverty and meanness. To avoid similar entanglements, the course which Christian men must follow is this: first, they must not long for, or hope for, or think of any kind of prosperity apart from the blessing of God; on it they must cast themselves, and there safely and confidently recline. For, however much the carnal mind may seem sufficient for itself when in the pursuit of honour or wealth, it depends on its own industry and zeal, or is aided by the favour of men, it is certain that all this is nothing, and that neither intellect nor labour will be of the least avail, except in so far as the Lord prospers both. On the contrary, his blessing alone makes a way through all obstacles, and brings everything to a joyful and favourable issue. Secondly, though without this blessing we may be able to acquire some degree of fame and opulence (as we daily see wicked men loaded with honours and riches), yet since those on whom the curse of God lies do not enjoy the least particle of true happiness, whatever we obtain without his blessing must turn out ill. But surely men ought not to desire what adds to their misery.

Therefore, if we believe that all prosperous and desirable

success depends entirely on the blessing of God, and that when it is wanting all kinds of misery and calamity await us, it follows that we should not eagerly contend for riches and honours, trusting to our own dexterity and assiduity, or leaning on the favour of men, or confiding in any empty imagination of fortune; but should always have respect to the Lord, that under his auspices we may be conducted to whatever lot he has provided for us. First, the result will be, that instead of rushing on regardless of right and wrong, by wiles and wicked arts, and with injury to our neighbours, to catch at wealth and seize upon honours, we will only follow such fortune as we may enjoy with innocence. Who can hope for the aid of the divine blessing amid fraud, rapine, and other iniquitous arts? As this blessing attends him only who thinks purely and acts uprightly, so it calls off all who long for it from sinister designs and evil actions. Secondly, a curb will be laid upon us, restraining a too eager desire to becoming rich, or an ambitious striving after honour. How can any one have the effrontery to expect that God will aid him in accomplishing desires at variance with his word? What God with his own lips pronounces cursed, never can be prosecuted with his blessing. Lastly, if our success is not equal to our wish and hope, we shall, however, be kept from impatience and detestation of our condition, whatever it be, knowing that so to feel were to murmur against God, at whose pleasure riches and poverty, contempt and honours, are dispensed. In short, he who leans on the divine blessing in the way which has been described, will not, in the pursuit of those things which men are wont most eagerly to desire, employ wicked arts which he knows would avail him nothing; nor when any thing prosperous befalls him will he impute it to himself and his own diligence, or industry, or fortune, instead of ascribing it to God as its author. If, while the affairs of others flourish, his make little progress, or even retrograde, he will bear his humble lot with greater equanimity and moderation than any irreligious man does the moderate success which only falls short of what he wished; for he has a solace in which he can rest more tranquilly than at the very summit of wealth or power, because he considers that his affairs are ordered by the Lord in the manner most conducive to his salvation.

XVII

John Wesley, The use of money, Sermon L in *Sermons on Several Occasions*, 1825, Vol. I. p. 634.

You see the nature and extent of truly Christian prudence, so far as it relates to the use of that great talent, Money. Gain all you can, without hurting either yourself or your neighbour, in soul or body, by applying hereto with unintermitted diligence, and with all the understanding which God has given you;—Save all you can, by cutting off every expense which serves only to indulge foolish desire; to gratify either the desire of the flesh, the desire of the eye, or the pride of life; waste nothing, living or dying, on sin or folly, whether for yourself or your children;—and then, Give all you can, or, in other words, give all you have to God. Do not stint yourself, like a Jew rather than a Christian, to this or that proportion. Render unto God, not a tenth, not a third, not half, but all that is God's, be it more or less; by employing all, or yourself, your household, the household of faith, and all mankind, in such a manner that you may give a good account of your stewardship, when you can be no longer stewards; ...

I entreat you, in the name of the Lord Jesus Christ, act up to the dignity of your calling! No more sloth! Whatsoever your hand findeth to do, do it with your might! No more waste! Cut off every expense which fashion, caprice, or flesh and blood demand. No more covetousness! But employ whatever God has entrusted you with in doing good, all possible good, in every possible kind and degree, to the household of faith, to all men!

XVIII

George Herbert, 1593–1633.

Teach me, my God and King,
In all things Thee to see,
And what I do in anything
To do it as for Thee!

A man that looks on glass,
On it may stay his eye,
Or if he pleaseth, through it pass,
And then the heaven espy.

All may of Thee partake;
Nothing can be so mean,
Which, with this tincture, 'for Thy sake',
Will not grow bright and clean.

A servant with this clause
Makes drudgery divine:
Who sweeps a room, as for Thy laws,
Makes that and the action fine.

This is the famous stone
That turneth all to gold;
For that which God doth touch and own
Cannot for less be told.

XIX

Adam Smith, *The Wealth of Nations*, 1776, Everyman edition, Vol. II. pp. 246–50, 1910.

The endowments of schools and colleges have necessarily diminished more or less the necessity of application in the teachers. Their subsistence, so far as it arises from their salaries, is evidently derived from a fund altogether independent of their success and reputation in their particular professions.

In some universities the salary makes but a part, and frequently but a small part, of the emoluments of the teacher, of which the greater part arises from the honoraries or fees of his pupils. The necessity of application, though always more or less diminished, is not in this case entirely taken away. Reputation in his profession is still of some importance to him, and he still has some dependency upon the affection, gratitude and favourable report of those who have attended upon his instructions; and these favourable sentiments he is likely to gain in no way so well as by deserving them, that is, by the abilities and diligence with which he discharges every part of his duty.

In other universities the teacher is prohibited from receiving any honorary or fee from his pupils, and his salary constitutes the whole of the revenue which he derives from his office. His interest is, in this case, set as directly in opposition to his duty as it is possible to set it. It is the interest of every man to live as much at his ease as he can; and if his emoluments are to be precisely the same, whether he does or does not perform some very laborious duty, it is certainly his interest, at least as interest is vulgarly understood, either to neglect it altogether, or, if he is subject to some authority which will not suffer him to do this, to perform it in as careless and slovenly a manner as that authority will permit. If he is naturally active and a lover of labour, it is his interest to employ that activity in any way from which he can derive some advantage, rather than in the performance of his duty, from which he can derive none.

If the authority to which he is subject resides in the body corporate, the college, or university, of which he himself is a member, and in which the greater part of the other members are, like himself, persons who either are or ought to be teachers, they are likely to make a common cause, to be all very indulgent to one another, and every man to consent that his neighbour may neglect his duty, provided he himself is allowed to neglect his own. In the university of Oxford, the greater part of the public professors have, for these many years, given up altogether even the pretence of teaching.

If the authority to which he is subject resides, not so much in the body corporate of which he is a member, as in some other extraneous persons—in the bishop of the diocese, for example; in the governor of the province; or, perhaps, in some minister of state—it is not indeed in this case very likely that he will be suffered to neglect his duty altogether. All that such superiors, however, can force him to do, is to attend upon his pupils a certain number of hours, that is, to give a certain number of lectures in the week or in the year. What those lectures shall be must still depend upon the diligence of the teacher; and that diligence is likely to be proportioned to the motives which he has for exerting it. An extraneous jurisdiction of this kind, besides, is liable to be exercised both ignorantly and capriciously. In its nature it is arbitrary and discretionary, and the persons who exercise it, neither attending upon the lectures of the teacher themselves, nor perhaps understanding the sciences which it is his business to teach, are seldom capable of exercising it with judgment. From the insolence of office, too, they are frequently indifferent how they exercise it, and are very apt to censure or deprive him of his office wantonly, and without any just cause. The person subject to such jurisdiction is necessarily degraded by it, and, instead of being one of the most respectable, is rendered one of the meanest and most contemptible persons in the society. It is by powerful protection only that he can effectually guard himself against the bad usage to which he is at all times exposed; and this protection he is most likely to gain, not by ability or diligence in his profession, but by obsequiousness to the will of his superiors, and by being ready, at all times, to sacrifice to that will the rights, the interest, and the honour of the body corporate of which he is a member. Whoever has attended for any considerable time to the administration of a French university must have had occasion to remark the effects which naturally result from an arbitrary and extraneous jurisdiction of this kind.

Whatever forces a certain number of students to any college or university, independent of the merit or reputation of the teachers, tends more or less to diminish the necessity of that merit or reputation. . . .

The discipline of colleges and universities is in general contrived, not for the benefit of the students, but for the interest, or more properly speaking, for the ease of the masters. Its object is, in all cases, to maintain the authority of the master, and whether he neglects or performs his duty, to oblige the students in all cases to behave to him as if he performed it with the greatest diligence and ability. It seems to presume perfect wisdom and virtue in the one order, and the greatest weakness and folly in the other. Where the masters, however, really perform their duty, there are no examples, I believe, that the greater part of the students ever neglect theirs. No discipline is ever requisite to force attendance upon lectures which are really worth the attending, as is well known wherever any such lectures are given. Force and restraint may, no doubt, be in some degree requisite in order to oblige children, or very young boys, to attend to those parts of education which it is thought necessary for them to acquire during that early period of life; but after twelve or thirteen years of age, provided the master does his duty, force or restraint can scarce ever be necessary to carry on any part of education. Such is the generosity of the greater part of young men, that, so far from being disposed to neglect or despise the instructions of their master, provided he shows some serious intention of being of use to them, they are generally inclined to pardon a great deal of incorrectness in the performance of his duty, and sometimes even to conceal from the public a good deal of gross negligence.

Those parts of education, it is to be observed, for the teaching of which there are no public institutions, are generally the best taught. When a young man goes to a fencing or a dancing school, he does not indeed always learn to fence or to dance very well;

but he seldom fails of learning to fence or to dance. The good effects of the riding school are not commonly so evident. The expense of a riding school is so great, that in most places it is a public institution. The three most essential parts of literary education, to read, write, and account, it still continues to be more common to acquire in private than in public schools; and it very seldom happens that anybody fails of acquiring them to the degree in which it is necessary to acquire them.

In England the public schools are much less corrupted than the universities. In the schools the youth are taught, or at least may be taught, Greek and Latin; that is, everything which the masters pretend to teach, or which, it is expected, they should teach. In the universities the youth neither are taught, nor always can find any proper means of being taught, the sciences which it is the business of those incorporated bodies to teach. The reward of the schoolmaster in most cases depends principally, in some cases almost entirely, upon the fees or honoraries of his scholars. Schools have no exclusive privileges. In order to obtain the honours of graduation, it is not necessary that a person should bring a certificate of his having studied a certain number of years at a public school. If upon examination he appears to understand what is taught there, no questions are asked about the place where he learnt it.

XX

William Alexander, Report on the Western District of Scotland, in *Report of Inspectors of Coal Mines, 1860.* Parliamentary Papers, 1861, XXII. pp. 145–6.

The safe and economical working of mines depends very much upon the ability of the person intrusted with the management, and any scheme, the object of which is to raise the standard or qualifications of underground managers, cannot but have a beneficial effect upon mining generally.

The School of Mines in Glasgow has been established solely with this view; it has been in operation for the past year, and the annual examination took place on the 14th of November last.

The students on the occasion made a most respectable appearance, and from the ready and off-hand way in which they replied to the questions put by those present in matters relating to the practical working of and management of mines, it was evident that they were quite conversant with the various subjects to which their attention had been directed during the session . . .

Certificates of merit were granted to a few of those who had most distinguished themselves in mechanical drawing, and in a knowledge of the various branches relating to practical mine engineering professed during the session.

The examination excited considerable interest, and some of the leading employees, in addition to their liberal subscriptions, intimated before leaving the room that prizes would be given at the next examination.

The Committee appointed by the subscribers to overlook the working of the school report

"That the attendance throughout the session has exceeded their expectations. Five-sixths of the students are workmen engaged in and about the mines, who, at considerable sacrifice and inconvenience to themselves, have been constant in their attendance, affording a very satisfactory proof of the wish for instruction by that class of men.

"In conclusion, the Committee are happy to be able to congratulate the subscribers on the success which has attended this the first session of the Glasgow School of Mines. The progress and success of such an institution is of vast importance to this and every mining district, for not only will it tend to raise the science of mine management, but ultimately lead to the elevation and improvement of those 'hardy sons of toil', the produce of whose labour is every day becoming more important and valuable for the support and prosperity of this great manufacturing country."

The funds are raised by voluntary contributions from the coal and iron masters, mineral proprietors, and gentlemen interested in the success of mining generally; and the scale of charges has been fixed for workmen at 6d. per week, and for others not relying upon their own efforts for support six guineas per annum.

XXI

William Alexander, Report on the Western District of Scotland, in *Report of Inspectors of Mines, 1864.* Parliamentary Papers, 1865, XX. p. 145.

It is to be regretted that the Glasgow School of Mines, which existed for nearly five years, has, for want of support, been closed since July last. Such an institution, designed for the improvement of workmen practically acquainted with the minutiae of mining, and where they might acquire the groundwork of mining engineering, could scarcely fail to prove beneficial to a mining district.

It had the effect of dissipating prejudice, and spreading a general knowledge of the various modes of working, and the schemes introduced from time to time to economize labour, or meet the peculiarities of local districts. As it is, improvements travel slowly, and not infrequently important ones are practised for a considerable time in one colliery before they are introduced into the work adjoining.

XXII

Evidence of John Young, Professor of Natural History in Glasgow University, 23 February 1872, to the *Royal Commission of Scientific Instruction*. Parliamentary Papers, 1874, XXII, Qq. 9591, 9593, 9602, 9603, 9609.

Have these defects to which you have alluded had any prejudicial consequences upon the profession of civil engineering ?—I believe that they do with the unfitness of the men from my point of view, when they enter upon the study of civil engineering; that is to say, that there has been no encouragement in the elementary schools, that there have not been competent teachers, even supposing that there had been encouragement, and that consequently men come to the Universities to learn what they ought to have learnt elsewhere; and as to the teachers we never reach to the higher grades of our subject, simply because we should be talking over their heads if we attempted it . . .

To what class are the popular lectures in the Andersonian and Mechanics' Institution addressed ?—There is no special definition of the class as regards the Andersonian University, but the Mechanics' Institution, as its title implies, was primarily intended for workmen. In both cases the present auditors are not workmen, but men in the position of clerks, foremen, and the upper classes altogether of the working community, men in receipt of income from probably 100£. to 150£. or 200£. . . .

. . . Lately an attempt has been made to establish a degree of science under the title of Bachelor of Science . . . The degree has been established in three departments, in law, in natural science, and in engineering science. In natural science there are two courses, one in biological science and the other in geological science, and as regards those two . . . my regret is that . . . the requirements in the direction of arts are far too great. Thus in biological science there are five subjects stated, namely, chemistry, anatomy, physiology, zoology, and botany, the candidate having it in his power to select any four of them, and four classes in the arts curriculum. In geological science he may select geology, chemistry, zoology, and the higher natural philosophy, with four classes in the arts curriculum, and the option of geodesy at the hands of the Professor of Astronomy. The requirement of four classes in the arts curriculum seems to me and to others to be somewhat excessive, taking into consideration the fact which the Universities must not now lose sight of, namely that men enter upon the profession of science in very different spirit to what they did many years ago. We must remember that many enter upon it purely as a trade, if one might use that word without disparagement. I have no other phrase to convey the idea. It is all very well for the Universities to say, Yes, but we must secure a higher standard of education from those men. If the Universities stand upon that ground they will soon be left high and dry and the whole scientific education of the country will drift past them. Other sources of instruction will arise, and the Universities will cease to take part in the general scientific instruction of the people . . .

Your impression is . . . that improvements such as you contemplated are not at present to be expected to originate in local intelligence or liberality?—Exceptional liberality may be met with; but where you have to deal with a very large number of proprietors, as I have in Lanarkshire, men of various social positions, I find that there is not a sufficient appreciation of the practical benefits of scientific teaching. In fact, remarks which were made to me by men of very good positions as regards wealth showed that they were utterly unfit to appreciate the direct benefit to themselves of such courses as I proposed; and I attribute this defective comprehension simply to the fact that our elementary and even our secondary schools do not distribute through the people a sufficient amount of scientific instruction.

Taking the managers of the large collieries and ironworks of Lanarkshire, what proportion of them have had elementary scientific training, either in an elementary or in any secondary school, and what proportion of them have fitted themselves, by independent self-sustained studies, to pass an elementary examination in science?—A very small number indeed. I should not like to say that there were none, but a very small number indeed are properly qualified to undertake the duties that are at present committed to them. They have a routine practice, and I quite admit that the pit or the workshop is the best place for learning a certain amount of their duty; but beyond the rule of thumb that they have learnt they are perfectly incompetent to deal with anything that may arise. In any emergency they are helpless; they are obliged to consult a civil engineer or a mining engineer and as I have already said, the majority of the civil and the mining engineers are not in a position to give them certain assistance . . .

Do artizans in Scotland practically make any use of the University of Glasgow?—None whatever. I have referred to my assistant in the matter of mining. He attended the medical classes during his first two winters, and during the intervening summer he returned to the pit and wrought in the pit, thereby procuring sufficient money to carry him on for the rest of his course, and he is now a very distinguished member of the profession; but those are exceptional cases altogether. One may say that they almost prove the rule that artizans do not avail themselves of the University.

XXIII

Robert Owen, *Report to the County of Lanark*, 1820, Pelican Classics Edition, 1969, pp. 249–52.

Your Reporter, in educating the rising generation within his influence, has long adopted principles different from those which are usually acted upon.

He considers all children as beings whose dispositions, habits, and sentiments are to be formed *for* them; that these can be well-formed only by excluding all notions of reward, punishment, and emulation; and that, if their characters are not such as they ought to be, the error proceeds from their instructors and the other circumstances which surround them. He knows that principles as certain as those upon which the science of mathematics is founded may be applied to the forming of any given general character, and that by the influence of other circumstances, not a few individuals only, but the whole population of the world, may in a few years be rendered a very far superior race of beings to any now upon the earth, or which has been made known to us by history.

The children in these new schools should be therefore trained systematically to acquire useful knowledge through the means of sensible signs, by which their powers of reflection and judgement may be habituated to draw accurate conclusions from the facts presented to them. This mode of instruction is founded in nature, and will supersede the present defective and tiresome system of book learning, which is ill-calculated to give either pleasure or instruction to the minds of children. When arrangements founded on these principles shall be judiciously formed and applied to practice, children will, with ease and delight to themselves, acquire more real knowledge in a day, than they have yet attained under the old system in many months. They will not only thus acquire valuable knowledge, but the best habits and dispositions will be at the same time imperceptibly created in every one; and they will be trained to fill every office and to perform every duty that the well-being of their associates and the establishments can require. It is only by education, rightly understood, that communities of men can ever be well governed, and by means of such education every object of human society will be attained with the least labour and the most satisfaction.

It is obvious that training and education must be viewed as intimately connected with the employments of the association. The latter, indeed, will form an essential part of education under these arrangements. Each association, generally speaking, should create for itself a full supply of the usual necessaries, conveniences, and comforts of life.

The dwelling-houses and domestic arrangements being placed as near the centre of the land to be cultivated as circumstances will permit, it is concluded that the most convenient situation for the gardens will be adjoining the houses on the outside of the square; that these should be bounded by the principal roads; and that beyond them, at a sufficient distance to be covered by a plantation, should be placed the workshops and manufactory.

All will take their turn at some one or more of the occupations in this department, aided by every improvement that science can afford, alternately with employment in agriculture and gardening.

It has been a popular opinion to recommend a minute division of labour and a division of interests. It will presently appear, however, that this minute division of labour and division of interests are only other terms for poverty, ignorance, waste of every kind, universal opposition throughout society, crime, misery, and great bodily and mental imbecility.

To avoid these evils, which, while they continue, must keep mankind in a most degraded state, each child will receive a general education, early in life, that will fit him for the proper purposes of society, make him the most useful to it, and the most capable of enjoying it.

Before he is twelve years old he may with ease be trained to acquire a correct view of the outline of all the knowledge which men have yet attained.

By this means he will early learn what he is in relation to past ages, to the period in which he lives, to the circumstances in which he is placed, to the individuals around him, and to future

8—EIB * *

events. He will then only have any pretensions to the name of a rational being.

His physical powers may be equally enlarged, in a manner as beneficial to himself as to those around him. As his strength increases he will be initiated in the practice of all the leading operations of his community, by which his services, at all times and under all circumstances, will afford a great gain to society beyond the expense of his subsistence; while at the same time he will be in the continual possession of more substantial comforts and real enjoyments than have ever yet appertained to any class in society.

The new wealth which one individual, by comparatively light and always healthy employment, may create under the arrangements now proposed, is indeed incalculable. They would give him giant powers compared with those which the working class or any other now possesses. There would at once be an end of all mere animal machines, who could only follow a plough, or turn a sod, or make some insignificant part of some insignificant manufacture or frivolous article which society could better spare than possess. Instead of the unhealthy pointer of a pin,—header of a nail,—piever of a thread—or clodhopper, senselessly gazing at the soil or around him, without understanding or rational reflection, there would spring up a working class full of activity and useful knowledge, with habits, information, manners, and dispositions, that would place the lowest in the scale many degrees above the best of any class which has yet been formed by the circumstances of past or present society.

Such are a few only of the advantages which a rational mode of training and education, combined with the other parts of this system, would give to all the individuals within the action of its influence.

XXIV

Report by T. Tancred on the Employment of Children and Young Persons in the Collieries and Ironworks of the West of Scotland. *Children's Employment Commission,* Mines and Collieries, Report of Sub-commissioner, Part I, Parliamentary Papers, 1842, XVI, pp 314–5.

A Works School

The plan of inducing the parents to send their children to school at these works and at Calder Bank (both belonging to the Monkland Iron Company) is peculiar, and is said to work well. Every adult male employed at the works, and residing within a mile of them, is required to contribute 2d. weekly to the maintenance of schools. This payment entitles him to send one child (either his own or a neighbour's) to any of the schools supported by the works, either day or night school; and if he sends more than one of his own children, he pays 1d. a-week extra for each. The several schoolmasters meet once a-week, and send into the pay office their lists of scholars, receiving for each the 2d. or 1d. per week, and the surplus at the end of the half-year is divided amongst them in proportion to the number of their scholars. The school-houses, fires, and dwellings for the masters, are furnished by the company. The attendance of children up to a certain age was very numerous under this plan. Indeed, one school which I visited was most improperly crowded—it was really impossible to get in at the door; and on surveying the dense mass of children within they appeared to be standing on each other's shoulders—one class who were reading having to stand upon the forms amongst the writers, the floor being too crowded to allow for their remaining upon it. This will appear no exaggeration when it is stated that in a room 16 feet square and 9 feet high there were crammed 140 children of both sexes. This allows not 2 square feet of floor to each child; whereas the *minimum* allowed in national schools in England is 6 square feet. The 140 children occupied 256 square feet of floor, whilst the *National Society's* allowance would have been at least 840. There were no play ground but the road. The deleterious effects of this dreadfully crowded state of the school on both master and children need hardly be remarked. The former said that he had been lately laid up for a fortnight, chiefly, he believed, from being so many hours daily in an impure atmosphere. Very few works which I visited could be supposed so injurious to the health of the children as this school-room; and I am afraid very many of these buildings, if not so bad as the one I have alluded to, are very deficient in proper means of ventilation.

XXV

Education Commission (Scotland), 1866. Report on the State of Education in the County Districts of Scotland. p. 47.

In 1841 [the population of Dalry in Ayrshire] numbered 4791; in 1851, 8865; in 1861, 11,150, and it is now computed to be above 12,000. In these years it has ceased to be an ordinary county parish, and has become, in the minister's (Mr Stevenson) words, 'a rural monster', but under his benevolent despotism the educational requirements have been fully satisfied. There are eleven schools in the parish, with 2,091 children on the rolls, and of these, nine including the parish school, are under his superintendence, and most of them have been built at his instigation. The heritors erected a new parish school, the kirk-session opened or furnished four schools in necessitous districts, and Messrs Merry and Cunningham, the proprietors of the mines and ironworks, have co-operated liberally with his endeavours. Seven of these schools are aided by Government to the extent of nearly £400 annually, and the parochial school is inferior to very few in Scotland. At the last inspection, out of 215 children presented in the different standards, 213 passed in reading, 212 in writing, and 212 in arithmetic. Thirty-two scholars were learning Latin, twenty-two French, and fourteen mathematics. The other inspected schools are efficiently conducted, the buildings are good, the attendance on the whole, considering the character of the population, is good, and the management is admirable. There is a small district of hill country containing seven or eight farms at some distance from any school. But there is no deficiency in the education of the residents in that district. The children are conveyed to school, sometimes at considerable inconvenience, by their parents, who are among the best educated among the parishioners.

XXVI

Micklethwaite Mss. *1138/197-235*, John Rylands University Library, Manchester.

LETTER 1

Dronfield Academy,
9 November 1822

My dear Father,[1]
   I remit to you a few lines in hopes they will find you in a good state of Health as they leave me at present be pleased to send me a Parcel and some money for I am very much in want of the one thing needfull give my best respects to all my friends and Neighbours and let me know how my Brother Wllm. is and please write again as soon as possible and so no more at present. From

Your
Affectionate Son
Thomas Micklethwait

LETTER 2   [Draft reply to above on same sheet]

My dear Thomas,
   I duly recd. both your Letters but have been so much engaged that I fear you will think I have quiet forgot/deserted you. I can

---

   [1] Thomas Micklethwaite was a member of a South Yorkshire landed family which had close connections with the Leeds cloth trade throughout the eighteenth century. He had succeeded to the family estates but still retained business interests in Leeds and Wakefield in the 1820's. He and two brothers had dissolved partnership as cloth merchants in 1796 after years of wrangling. Almost thirty years later Thomas Micklethwaite was a very bitter man, now a widower and still at war with almost all his family. See Burke's *Landed Gentry* (1952 ed) and R. G. Wilson *Gentlemen Merchants* (1971), pp. 68–9.

assure you I have no intention to desert you if you will be a good boy diligent to learn and obediant to your Teachers and Masters always speak truth and cheerfully do as you are ordered and directed. I am at a loss to conceive why you are so urgent for Money as Mr. Butterman would pay you three pence a week which I think would be quite plenty to spend in these difficult times, Farming is a very loosing Trade and present, so you must learn to be Carefull and spend no more than you can help and in time you will feel good Effect of Economy and [word illegible] of your wants, do not exceed your Income. Xmas Vacation will soon be at hand when I shall expect to see you. Let me know a few days before and I will order Mr. Broadbent to pay your Coach I will go or send to you at Barnsley.

LETTER 3

Dronfield Academy,
1 *February*, 1823

Dear Father,

I have got the opportunity of writing to you a few lines in hope they will find you in good Health as it leaves me at Present. But as I was coming to Dronfield the last time I was verry sick and Picked up But when I got to Dronfield I was ill it was with Riding in the Coach and I hope my Brother Wllm. as got safe to school But why have [you] forgot my Dictionary and Black Lead Pensil which I am fast for they are in the wite table drawer in first kiching where my books was. If you will have the Trouble to send them me in a Parcil . . . . . and you must send me some Oranges Give my Respects to Mr. and Mrs. Smith no more at Present from

Your dutiful sone
T. Micklethwaite

Note scribbled "Sent by Express Coach the 11 Feb. 6 Oranges and Book etc."

LETTER 4

15 *March* 1823   *Dronfield Academy*
  I remit to you a few lines in hopes that they may find you in
good Health as it leaves me at Present But all that I have to write
to you for is that I think there is some thing the matter with you I
think so because that you did not Answer my last letter and
Easter is very near and I should wish to hear from you as soon as
possible because I think that I shall go to Chatsworth after Easter
becase all the boys that as a mind may go and I think that I shall
go But I should wish to hear from you as soon as possible I should
wish to hear from you this week Give my Respects to all my friends
and Neighbours, belive in me
                              Your affectionate son
                              T. Micklethwait

LETTER 5   [Draft reply to above]

23 *March, Ardsley*
My Dear Thomas,
  I was very glad to hear you got your Book and Oranges safe by
the Express. You mention having seen that Richard [his cousin of
New Laithes Grange, Leeds] was dead. He dyed in Consequence
of his own imprudence by Drinking and dissipation—which is a
very lamentable thing that a young Man of 27 years died so early. I
see by your last letter you wish to go to Chatsworth, I have no
objection if you have a convenient and favourable opportunity of
going. I believe it is a most Magnificent Place and well worth
seeing, but I fear you are too young to derive much satisfaction
from such a place. However you must endeavour to make the best
remarks you can of the grander of the House, the Magnitude of
the Domaine, the Extent of the Park, Pleasure grounds and
gardens, stables etc. so as to be able to give me some account of
them when I have the pleasure to see you next.
                              I Remain,
                              Your most affectionately,
                              John Micklethwaite.

LETTER 6

Dronfield Academy
27 November 1824

My Dear Father,

   As it is now very near Xmas I thought it not amis to inform
you about Coming Home the week after next as there is a very
good Conveyance and Two weeks are no Portion of Time but still
they seem long. You talk off the Barnsly Linen Trade I think it
will suit me as well as anything for I wish you would put me to
some Business. I have got on this half-year as fast as Possible and
hope when you have the pleasure of seeing me next at Ardsley my
learning may meet with your approbation and the next half year I
may become a tolerable Accountant. You would perhaps wonder
how I can spend my Money without spending it to some use, I
have Letter Sheets, Knives, Quills, Paper to Cover my Books and
a Comb to buy, Letters to Loose [?] Parcels to pay for These will
soon Amount to four or five shillings. I should very much like to
hear from you as early as possible to know when I am to come
Home as you can meet me at Barnsley with the Mare, But
perhaps you will not have anybody to send with her as will know
me but if they put her into Broadbents stable I shall know where
to find her as I shall look into the Stable as soon as I get off a
Coach. You must write a few lines and say that I must be at
Barnsley on Thursday by the Express Coach. You must be sure
and write 5 or 6 lines to say the day I must Come Home on and
let that Day be Thursday, be sure and write 5 or 6 line and I shall
expect the Mare at Barnsly. We break up on the 16th and All the
Boys are gone on Saturday the 18th. I shall expect a letter the
next week without fail. No more at present.

From
Your dutiful son
T. Micklethwait.

LETTER 7

Dronfield Academy
3 May 1825

My dear Father,

Your kindness in placing me in a situation of this kind where I have such an extensive Opportunity for Improvement demands my most grateful Acknowledgements, and I assure you it would be a source of peculiar delight to find that my Exertions in the pursuit of useful Information are entitled to your Approbation. The Recess will commerce on the 18th Instant on which Day or the 17th with your Permission I propose visiting Home. I beg you will be kind enough to present my Respects where due and believe me

Your dutiful son
T. Micklethwaite

LETTER 8

Dronfield Academy
25 May 1825

Dear Father

It is with the greatest of pleasure that I embrace this letter to you hoping on the 15th or 16th of next Month to find you in Health, also happy and Comfortable in your fresh situation [Micklethwaite senior had just moved house].

I have made the most of my time this half year and hope when you see me at Midsummer my improvement will suit your approbation. You must be so kind as to let me have a Letter in a short time and inform me if you will meet me at Barnsley

We break up on the 15th and 16th

I think I have nothing of great importance to Communicate only to request a letter from you give my respects to all friends and Relations and

I remain dear Father
Your dutiful and affectionate son
Thomas Micklethwaite

LETTER 9   [Draft reply to above]

Dear Thomas,
   I duly read your hasty careless letter of 25th May. I say hastly
and careless because you finish abruptly and careless because you
write and block out. I shall be happy to find that you verify your
assertion of having made the best use of your time this half year
and you improvement will be found very considerable. I shall be
glad to see you here at the vacation . . . I have settled at Birkhouse
about a fortnight I don't dislike the situation I hope I shall make
it comfortable in time and I am in hast preparing to go to Leeds
on very particular Business and I remain
                    Dear Thomas,
               Yours most affectionately
                  John Micklethwaite

LETTER 10

                                              5 December 1825
My Dear Father,
   Although the Peculiarity of my situation be such as to create in
the Mind Sensations extremely oppisite; yet it is scarcely to be
conceived how powerfully Nature operates and often I think of
Home then at the same time I am anxious to divest my Thoughts
of it I have attended to such parts of Learning as are most likely
to be practically useful and as we have great Opportunities of
Improvement here; I flatter myself that my Progress will equal
the Expectation of all My friends. Our recess will commence the
17th Instant prior to which Period I shall be happy to hear from
you, and remain with Duty to you and Love to all dear Friends
                    Your dutiful son
                  Thomas Micklethwaite

LETTER II

Dronfield
31 *August* 1826

Dear Father,

I take the first opportunity of writing to you a few lines [as we have an Holyday today] hoping you are in good Health as I myself and all the School Boys are, I am getting on as fast as possible with my Landsurveying and hope by Xmas to become a tolerable Accountant. I am determined to make the most of my time this half year knowing it to be my last. As to what situation of life I may be placed in I hope to make myself useful. I think a Linen Manufacturer would suit but any thing that will do for you will suit me, I am only telling you what I think about it.

I shall be very happy to hear from you respecting my situation in life and if Mr. Butterman may let me have a Case of Instruments or Box of compasses as I cannot do without and have always to borrow from those who do not like to lend the reason Mr. B. will not let me have a Case is he *always* says I had better acquaint you as the Boys he has let have before and their Parent not knowing having not been pleased.

When I say a Case of Instruments I mean Compasses Scales and various other Articles on purpose to draw Plans and Figures etc. The number of Scholars this half year are 51. I shall expect a letter from you in a Short time.

and I remain
Your affectionate Son
Thomas Micklethwaite

LETTER 12   [Draft reply]

13 *September* 1826

Dear Thomas,

I am so much engaged in mind and Deed with [abbreviation illegible] and other matters that I have not time/leisure to think of your destination at present but I hope you will do as you promise by learning all you possibly can this last half year of your

Scholling. You say may Mr. B let me have a Case of Instruments of Box of Compasses It I suppose is one and the same thing. I think a scale and Comp. may always be useful to you if you take any delight in Drawing. You had better have a small useful case

LETTER 13

Rawmarsh Academy
10 *May* 1827

Dear Father,

It is with the greatest of pleasure that I write this letter to you to inform you that I have enjoyed good health and I hope you have enjoyed the same inestimable blessing at Birk House.

I am greatly obliged to you for all your favours. All that I have to hope is that the progress I make in my learning will be no disagreeable return for the same. Gratitude, duty and a view of future advantages all contribute to make me thoroughly sensible how much I ought to labour for my own improvement and if I neglect the opportunity and time it will never return and therefore I ought to embrace it with eagerness

I hope you will let Thomas come over to Rawmarsh some day and bring me a few apples.

I am dear Father,
Your ever dutiful and obedient son
Wllm Micklethwaite

P.S. I am in want of a pair of shose for when Summer comes I canot wear my boots I want to know if I must get them and save my boots for winter

LETTER 14   [Draft reply to the above]

Dear William,

I was much pleased with your indited letter. If you only act as you write and Labor for Improvement I hope you will become an usefull Member of Society. I am sorry the apples are all done and Thomas remains very Indolent . . .

XXVII

A. Marshall, *Principles of Economics*, 8th edn., 1920. pp. 298–300.

It is obvious that the son of a man already established in business starts with very great advantages over others. He has from his youth up special facilities for obtaining the knowledge and developing the faculties that are required in the management of his father's business: he learns quietly and almost unconsciously about men and manners in his father's trade and in those from which that trade buys and to which it sells; he gets to know the relative importance and the real significance of the various problems and anxieties which occupy his father's mind: and he acquires a technical knowledge of the processes and the machinery of the trade. Some of what he learns will be applicable only to his father's trade; but the greater part will be serviceable in any trade that is in any way allied with that; while those general faculties of judgement and resource, of enterprise and caution, of firmness and courtesy, which are trained by association with those who control the larger issues of any one trade, will go a long way towards fitting him for managing almost any other trade. Further, the sons of successful business men start with more material capital than almost anyone else except those who by nurture and education are likely to be disinclined for business and unfitted for it; and if they continue their father's work, they have also the vantage ground of established trade connections.

It would therefore at first sight seem likely that business men should constitute a sort of caste; dividing out among their sons the chief posts of command, and founding hereditary dynasties, which should rule certain branches of trade for many generations together. But the actual state of things is very different. For when a man has got together a great business, his descendants often fail, in spite of their great advantages, to develop the high abilities and the special turn of mind and temperament required for carrying it on with equal success. He himself was probably brought up by parents of strong earnest character; and was educated by their personal influence and by struggle with difficulties in early life. But his children, at all events if they were born after he became rich, and in any case his grandchildren are perhaps left a good deal to the care of domestic servants who are not of the same strong fibre as the parents by whose influence he was educated. And while his highest ambition was probably success in business, they are likely to be at least equally anxious for social or academic distinction.

For a time indeed all may go well. His sons find a firmly established trade connection, and what is perhaps even more important, a well-chosen staff of subordinates with a generous interest in the business. By mere assiduity and caution, availing themselves of the traditions of the firm, they may hold together for a long time. But when a full generation has passed, when the old traditions are no longer a safe guide, and when the bonds that held together the old staff have been dissolved, then the business almost invariably falls to pieces unless it is practically handed over to the management of new men who have meanwhile risen to partnership in the firm.

But in most cases his descendants arrive at this result by a shorter route. They prefer an abundant income coming to them without effort on their part, to one which though twice as large could be earned only by incessant toil and anxiety; and they sell the business to private persons or a joint-stock company; or they become sleeping partners in it; that is sharing in its risks and its profits, but not taking part in its management: in either case the active control over their capital falls chiefly into the hands of new men.

XXVIII

Adam Smith, *The Wealth of Nations*, 1776, Everyman edition, Vol. II. pp. 198-9, 1910.

Among nations of hunters, as there is scarce any property, or at least none that exceeds the value of two or three days' labour, so there is seldom any established magistrate or any regular administration of justice. Men who have no property can injure one another only in their persons or reputations. But when one man kills, wounds, beats, or defames another, though he to whom the injury is done suffers, he who does it receives no benefit. It is otherwise with the injuries to property. The benefit of the person who does the injury is often equal to the loss of him who suffers it. Envy, malice, or resentment are the only passions which can prompt one man to injure another in his person or reputation. But the greater part of men are not very frequently under the influence of those passions, and the very worse men are so only occasionally. As their gratification too, how agreeable soever it may be to certain characters, is not attended with any real or permanent advantage, it is in the greater part of men commonly restrained by prudential considerations. Men may live together in society with some tolerable degree of security, though there is no civil magistrate to protect them from the injustice of those passions. But avarice and ambition in the rich, in the poor the hatred of labour and the love of present ease and enjoyment, are the passions which prompt to invade property, passions much more steady in their operation, and much more universal in their influence. Wherever there is great property there is great inequality. For one very rich man there must be at least five hundred poor, and the affluence of the few supposes the indigence of the many. The affluence of the rich excites the indignation of the poor, who are often both driven by want, and prompted by envy, to invade his possessions. It is only under the shelter of the civil magistrate that the owner of that valuable property, which is aquired by the labour of many years, or perhaps of many successive generations, can sleep a single night in security. He is at all times surrounded by unknown enemies, whom, though he never provoked, he can never appease, and from whose injustice he can be protected only by the powerful arm of the civil magistrate continually held up to chastise it. The acquisition of valuable and extensive property, therefore, necessarily requires the establishment of civil government. Where there is no property, or at least none that exeeds the value of two or three days' labour, civil government is not so necessary.

XXIX

Karl Marx and Friedrich Engels, *Manifesto of the Communist Party*, 1846, Progress Publishers, Moscow, 1965. pp. 43–7.

The bourgeoisie, historically, has played a most revolutionary part.

The bourgeoisie, wherever it has got the upper hand, has put an end to all feudal, patriarchal, idyllic relations. It has pitilessly torn asunder the motely feudal ties that bound man to his "natural superiors", and has left remaining no other nexus between man and man than naked self-interest, than callous "cash payment". It has drowned the most heavenly ecstasies of religious fervour, of chivalrous enthusiasm, of philistine sentimentalism, in the icy water of egotistical calculation. It has resolved personal worth into exchange value, and in place of the numberless indefeasible chartered freedoms, has set up that single, unconscionable freedom-Free Trade. In one word, for exploitation, veiled by religious and political illusions, it has substituted naked, shameless, direct, brutal exploitation.

The bourgeoisie has stripped of its halo every occupation hitherto honoured and looked up to with reverent awe. It has converted the physician, the lawyer, the priest, the poet, the man of science, into its paid wage-labourers.

The bourgeoisie has torn away from the family its sentimental veil, and has reduced the family relation to a mere money relation.

The bourgeoisie has disclosed how it came to pass that the brutal display of vigour in the Middle Ages, which Reactionists so much admire, found its fitting complement in the most slothful indolence. It has been the first to shew what man's activity can bring about. It has accomplished wonders far surpassing Egyptian pyramids, Roman aqueducts, and Gothic cathedrals; it has conducted expeditions that put in the shade all former Exoduses of nations and crusades.

The bourgeoisie cannot exist without constantly revolutionising the instruments of production, and thereby the relations of production, and with them the whole relations of society. Conservation of the old modes of production in unaltered form, was, on the contrary, the first condition of existence for all earlier industrial classes. Constant revolutionising of production, uninterrupted disturbance of all social conditions, everlasting uncertainty and agitation distinguish the bourgeois epoch from all earlier ones. All fixed, fast-frozen relations, with their train of ancient and venerable prejudices and opinions are swept away, all new-formed ones become antiquated before they can ossify. All that is solid melts into air, all that is holy is profaned, and man is at last compelled to face with sober senses, his real conditions of life, and his relations with his kind.

The need of a constantly expanding market for its products chases the bourgeoisie over the whole surface of the globe. It must nestle everywhere, settle everywhere, establish connexions everywhere.

The bourgeoisie has through its exploitation of the work market given a cosmopolitan character to production and consumption in every country. To the great chagrin of Reactionists, it has drawn from under the feet of industry the national ground on which it stood. All old-established national industries have been destroyed or are daily being destroyed. They are dislodged by new industries, whose introduction becomes a life and death question for all civilised nations, by industries that no longer work up indigenous raw material, but raw material drawn from the remotest zones; industries whose products are consumed, not only at home, but in every quarter of the globe. In place of the old wants, satisfied by the productions of the country, we find new wants, requiring for their satisfaction the products of distant lands and climes. In place of the old local and national seclusion and self-sufficiency, we have intercourse in every direction, universal inter-dependence of nations. And as in material, so also in intellectual production. The intellectual creations of individual nations become common property. National one-sidedness and narrow-mindedness become more and more impossible, and from the numerous national and local literatures, there arises a world literature.

The bourgeoisie, by the rapid improvement of all instruments of production, by the immensely facilitated means of communication, draws all, even the most barbarian, nations into civilisation. The cheap prices of its commodities are the heavy artillery with which it batters down all Chinese walls, with which it forces the barbarians' intensely obstinate hatred of foreigners to capitulate. It compels all nations, on pain of extinction, to adopt the bourgeois mode of production; it compels them to introduce what it calls civilisation into their midst, i.e., to become bourgeois themselves. In one word, it creates a world after its own image.

The bourgeoisie has subjected the country to the rule of the towns. It has created enormous cities, has greatly increased the urban population as compared with the rural, and has thus rescued a considerable part of the population from the idiocy of rural life. Just as it has made the country dependent on the towns, so it has made barbarian and semi-barbarian countries dependent on the civilised ones, nations of peasants on nations of bourgeois, the East on the West.

The bourgeoisie keeps more and more doing away with the scattered state of the population, of the means of production, and of property. It has agglomerated population, centralised means of production, and has concentrated property in a few hands. The necessary consequence of this was political centralisation. Independent, or but loosely connected, provinces with separate interests, laws, governments and systems of taxation, became lumped together into one nation, with one government, one code of laws, one national class-interest, one frontier and one customs-tariff.

The bourgeoisie, during its rule of scarce one hundred years, has created more massive and more colossal productive forces than have all preceding generations together. Subjection of Nature's forces to man, machinery, application of chemistry to industry and agriculture, steam-navigation, railways, electric telegraphs, clearing of whole continents for cultivation, canalisation of rivers, whole populations conjured out of the ground—what earlier century had even a presentiment that such productive forces slumbered in the lap of social labour?

We shall see then: the means of production and of exchange, on whose foundation the bourgeoisie built itself up, were generated in feudal society. At a certain stage in the development of these means of production and of exchange, the conditions under which feudal society produced and exchanged, the feudal organisation of agriculture and manufacturing industry, in one word, the feudal relations of property became no longer compatible with the already developed productive forces; they became so many fetters. They had to be burst asunder; they were burst asunder.

XXX

J. S. Mill, *On Liberty*, 1859, Everyman edition. pp. 127–31, 1910.

The despotism of custom is everywhere the standing hindrance to human advancement, being in unceasing antagonism to that disposition to aim at something better than customary, which is called, according to circumstances, the spirit of liberty, or that of progress or improvement. The spirit of improvement is not always a spirit of liberty, for it may aim at forcing improvements on an unwilling people; and the spirit of liberty, in so far as it resists such attempts, may ally itself locally and temporarily with the opponents of improvement; but the only unfailing and permanent source of improvement is liberty, since by it there are as many possible independent centres of improvement as there are individuals. The progressive principle, however, in either shape, whether as the love of liberty or of improvement, is antagonistic to the sway of Custom, involving at least emancipation from that yoke; and the contest between the two constitutes the chief interest of the history of mankind. The greater part of the world has, properly speaking, no history, because the despotism of Custom is complete. This is the case over the whole East. Custom is there, in all things, the final appeal; justice and right mean conformity to custom; the argument of custom no one, unless some tyrant intoxicated with power, thinks of resisting. And we see the result. Those nations must once have had originality; they did not start out of the ground populous, lettered, and versed in many of the arts of life; they made themselves all this, and were then the greatest and most powerful nations of the world. What are they now? The subjects or dependents of tribes whose forefathers wandered in the forests when theirs had magnificent palaces and gorgeous temples, but over whom custom exercised only a divided rule with liberty and progress. A people, it appears, may be progressive for a certain length of time, and then stop: when does it stop? When it ceases to possess individuality. If a similar change should befall the nations of Europe, it will not be in exactly the same shape: the despotism of custom with which these nations are threatened is not precisely stationariness. It proscribes singularity, but it does not preclude change, provided all change together. We have discarded the fixed costumes of our forefathers; every one must still dress like other people, but the fashion may change once or twice a year. We thus take care that when there is a change, it shall be for change's sake, and not from any idea of beauty or convenience; for the same idea of beauty or convenience would not strike all the world at the same moment, and be simultaneously thrown aside by all at another moment. But we are progressive as well as changeable: we continually make new inventions in mechanical things, and keep them until they are again superseded by better; we are eager for improvement in politics, in education, even in morals, though in this last our idea of improvement chiefly consists in persuading or forcing other people to be as good as ourselves. It is not progress that we object to; on the contrary, we flatter ourselves that we are the most progressive people who ever lived. It is individuality that we war against: we should think we had done wonders if we had made ourselves all alike; forgetting that the unlikeness of one person to another is generally the first thing which draws the attention of either to the imperfection of his own type, and the superiority of another, or the possibility, by combining the advantages of both, of producing something better than either. We have a warning example in China—a nation of much talent, and, in some respects, even wisdom, owing to the rare good fortune of having been provided at an early period with a particularly good set of customs, the work in some measure, of men to whom even the most enlightened European must accord, under certain limitations, the title of sages and philosophers. They are remarkable, too, in the excellence of their apparatus for impressing, as far as possible, the best wisdom they possess upon every mind in the community, and securing that those who have appropriated most of it shall occupy the posts of honour and power. Surely the people who did this have discovered the secret of human progressiveness, and must have kept themselves steadily at the head of the movement of the world. On the contrary, they have become stationary—have remained so for thousands of years; and if they are ever to be farther improved, it must be by foreigners. They have succeeded beyond all hope in what English philanthropists are so industriously working at—in making a people all alike, all governing their thoughts and conduct by the same maxims and rules; and these are the fruits. The modern *regime* of public opinion is, in an unorganised form, what the Chinese educational and political systems are in an organised; and unless individuality shall be able successfully to assert itself against this yoke, Europe, notwithstanding its notable antecedents and its professed Christianity, will tend to become another China.

What is it that has hitherto preserved Europe from this lot? What has made the European family of nations an improving, instead of a stationary portion of mankind? Not any superior excellence in them, which, when it exists, exists as the effect not as the cause; but their remarkable diversity of character and culture. Individuals, classes, nations, have been extremely unlike one another: they have struck out a great variety of paths, each leading to something valuable, and although at every period those who travelled in different paths have been intolerant of one another, and each would have thought it an excellent thing if all the rest could have been compelled to travel his road, their attempts to thwart each other's development have rarely had any permanent success, and each has in time endured to receive the good which the others have offered. Europe is, to my judgment, wholly indebted to this plurality of paths for its progressive and many-sided development. But it already begins to possess this benefit in a considerably less degree. It is decidedly advancing towards the Chinese ideal of making all people alike. The circumstances which surround different classes and individuals, and shape their characters, are daily becoming more assimilated. Formerly, different ranks, different neighbourhoods, different trades and professions, lived in what might be called different worlds; at present to a great degree in the same. Comparatively speaking, they now read the same things, listen to the same things, see the same things, go to the same places, have their hopes and fears directed to the same objects, have the same rights and liberties, and the same means of asserting them. Great as are the differences of position which remain, they are nothing to those which have ceased. And the assimilation is still proceeding. All the political changes of the age promote it, since they all tend to raise the low and to lower the high. Every extension of education promotes it, because education brings people under common influences, and gives them access to the general stock of facts and sentiments. Improvement in the means of communication promotes it, by bringing the inhabitants of distant places into personal contact, and keeping up a rapid flow of changes of residence between one place and another. The increase of commerce and manufactures promotes it, by diffusing more widely the advantages of easy circumstances, and opening all objects of ambition, even the highest, to general competition, whereby the desire of rising becomes no longer the character of a particular class, but of all classes. A more powerful agency than even all these, in bringing about a general similarity among mankind, is the complete establishment, in this and other free countries, of the ascendancy of public opinion in the State. As the various social eminences which enabled persons entrenched on them to disregard the opinion of the multitude gradually become levelled; as the very idea of resisting the will of the public, when it is positively known that they have a will, disappears more and more from the minds of practical politicians; there ceases to be any social support for nonconformity—any substantive power in society which, itself opposed to the ascendancy of numbers, is interested in taking under its protection opinions and tendencies at variance with those of the public.

XXXI

Samuel Johnson, *Journey to the Western Islands of Scotland*, 1775, Oxford Standard Authors ed. 1961. pp. 77–9.

The name of highest dignity is Laird, . . . The Laird is the original owner of the land, whose natural power must be very great, where no man lives but by agriculture; and where the produce of the land is not conveyed through the labyrinths of traffick, but passes directly from the hand that gathers it to the mouth that eats it. The Laird has all those in his power that live upon his farms. Kings can, for the most part, only exalt or degrade. The Laird at pleasure can feed or starve, can give bread, or withold it. This inherent power was yet strengthened by the kindness of consanguinity, and the reverence of patriarchal authority. The Laird was the father of the Clan, and his tenants commonly bore his name. And to these principles of original command was added, for many ages, an exclusive right of legal jurisdiction.

This multifarious, and extensive obligation operated with force scarcely credible. Every duty, moral or political, was absorbed in affection and adherence to the Chief. Not many years have passed since the clans knew no law but the Laird's will. He told them to whom they should be friends or enemies, what King they should obey, and what religion they should profess. . . .

Next in dignity to the Laird is the Tacksman; a large taker or leaseholder of land, of which he keeps part, as a domain, in his own hand, and lets part to under tenants. The Tacksman is necessarily a man capable of securing to the Laird the whole rent, and is commonly a collateral relation. These *tacks*, or subordinate possessions, were long considered as hereditary, and the occupant was distinguished by the name of the place at which he resided. He held a middle station, by which the highest and the lowest orders were connected. He paid rent and reverence to the Laird, and received them from the tenants. This tenure still subsists, with its original operation, but not with the primitive stability. Since the islanders, no longer content to live, have learned the desire of growing rich, an ancient dependent is in danger of giving way to a higher bidder, at the expense of domestick dignity and hereditary power. The stranger, whose money buys him preference, considers himself as paying for all that he has, and is indifferent about the Laird's honour or safety. The commodiousness of money is indeed great; but there are some advantages which money cannot buy, and which therefore no wise man will by the love of money be tempted to forego.

I have found in the hither parts of *Scotland*, men not defective in judgment or general experience, who consider the Tacksmen as a useless burden of the ground, as a drone who lives upon the product of an estate, without the right of property, or the merit of labour, and who impoverishes at once the landlord and the tenant. The land, say they, is let to the Tacksman at six-pence an acre, and by him to the tenant at ten-pence. Let the owner be the immediate landlord to all the tenants; if he sets the ground at eight-pence, he will increase his revenue by a fourth part, and the tenant's burthen will be diminished by a fifth.

Those who pursue this train of reasoning, seem not sufficiently to inquire whither it will lead them, nor to know that it will equally shew the propriety of suppressing all wholesale trade, of shutting up the shops of every man who sells what he does not make, and of extruding all whose agency and profit intervene between the manufacturer and the consumer. They may, by stretching their understandings a little wider, comprehend, that all those who by undertaking large quantities of manufacture, and affording employment to many labourers, make themselves considered as benefactors to the publick, have only been robbing their workmen with one hand, and their customers with the other. If Crowley had sold only what he could make, and all his smiths had wrought their own iron with their own hammers, he would have lived on less, and they would have sold their work for more. The salaries of superintendents and clerks would have been partly saved, and partly shared, and nails been sometimes cheaper by a farthing in a hundred. But then if the smith could not have found an immediate purchaser, he must have deserted his anvil; if there had by accident at any time been more sellers than buyers, the workmen must have reduced their profit to nothing, by underselling one another; and as no great stock could have been in any hand, no sudden demand of large quantities could have been answered, and the builder must have stood still till the nailer could supply him.

According to these schemes, universal plenty is to begin and end in universal misery. Hope and emulation will be utterly extinguished; and as all must obey the call of immediate necessity, nothing that requires extensive views, or provides for distant consequences, will ever be performed.

To the southern inhabitants of Scotland, the state of the Mountains and the islands is equally unknown with that of *Borneo* or *Sumatra*: Of both they have only heard a little, and guess the rest. They are strangers to the language and the manners, to the advantages and wants of the people whose life they would model, and whose evils they would remedy.

Nothing is less difficult than to procure one convenience by the forfeiture of another. A soldier may expedite his march by throwing away his arms. To banish the Tacksman is easy, to make a country plentiful by diminishing the people, is an expeditious mode of husbandry; but that abundance, which there is nobody to enjoy, contributes little to human happiness.

XXXII

E. R. Cregeen, The Changing Role of the House of Argyll in the Scottish Highlands, in I. M. Lewis, ed., *History and Social Anthropology*, 1968. pp. 167-9, 176-7.

The House of Argyll
and its New Entrepreneurial Role

In the eighteenth century the role of the Duke of Argyll in the Highlands is no longer in the political and religious spheres a revolutionary one. With the triumph of their cause through the events of 1688 and 1714, their role is that of maintaining the established order against Tories, papists, Jacobites, and the disaffected generally. They take the lead in destroying the threat from the Stuarts in 1715 and 1745.

But, true to their tradition as pioneers and innovators, they assume a new revolutionary role as leaders of economic and social change. They are found introducing agricultural improvements in the early decades of the eighteenth century. They revolutionize the whole basis of land tenure on their estate before 1740. They build a castle at Inveraray in the new Gothic style, one of the earliest examples of this fashion in Britain, and lay out parks, gardens, and woodlands. They build new towns and villages, found industries, promote the construction of roads, piers, and canals, and encourage schemes of re-settlement in the Highlands to prevent emigration. One after another, with remarkable consistency, the eighteenth-century dukes pursue this new economic policy, making Inveraray the main focus of change and 'improvement' in the West Highlands.

It was natural that the Argylls should assume a pioneer role. Their political activities made them normally resident in London, so that their visits to their Highland estates were usually confined to a few summer months. Their social activities, tastes, and expenditure were those of the great Whig magnates. The possession of five thousand fighting men as a personal following no doubt lent a certain romantic grandeur to the Duke of Argyll in the eyes of his peers, but the spending of five thousand pounds a year in cash was more necessary if the Duke was not to appear down at heel among the Russells, the Stanhopes, and the Pelhams. A perennial need for revenue characterized the estate management of the Dukes of Argyll in the eighteenth century.

The new economic role of the house of Argyll was in one sense an aspect of their more general political role. Although the execution of their programme of agrarian reorganization was sometimes, as will appear, in conflict with immediate political objectives, both stemmed from the same underlying philosophy. When, in his instructions to the Chamberlain of Tiree in 1756, the third Duke, requiring that tenants should henceforth pay a part of their rents in spun yarn and that their womenfolk should spin diligently, wrote: 'I'm resolved to keep no tenants but such as will be peaceable and apply themselves to industry. You'll cause intimate this same sobbath after sermon', he was speaking as a good Whig. In the schemes for 'civilizing the Highlands' which occupied the Duke and his friends in Government after 1745, projects for linen factories in remote areas, associated with the cultivation of flax and domestic spinning, bulked large. The economic virtues of hard work, thrift, and sobriety were constantly urged upon the Highlanders, and were regarded by the Duke and his friends as an excellent antidote to Jacobitism and disaffection, which thrived in idleness and intemperance.

The encouragement of such virtues, however, went beyond a purely political purpose. Industrious, sober, and enterprising tenants were required if the estate was to yield a steadily increasing rental. This would be beneficial not to the Duke alone, but also to the tenant. Thus, the fifth Duke, later in the century, when pursuing his programme of abolishing the joint farms, appealed to the spirit of private enterprise and wrote to the Chamberlain of Mull: 'My own wish is that these farms should be divided into sixteen different possessions so as every man may have his own separate farm to manage and improve in his own way, and the skilful and industrious may reap the benefit of their labours and knowledge, and at the same time be examples to others' . . .

———————

The alliance of Duke and vassals went beyond politics into economics. Enterprising Campbells initiated and promoted ducal improvements at Inveraray and over the estate at large. The almost hereditary positions which several ancient families occupied in the estate administration gave them influence over it. Innovations in animal breeding, agricultural practice, and tree-planting at Inveraray spread quickly to other estates in Argyll. Cattle of finer breed from the Duke's parks were, for example, sold chiefly to Campbell lairds with a view to improving the West Highland breed.

The Duke's new castle at Inveraray and his general style of life undoubtedly influenced the West Highland lairds. One notes the spread of a fashion for new country houses, parks, and other embellishments; for town houses, carriages, and servants in livery; for English and Lowland ways and often ruinous expense.

New enterprises, underwritten by the Duke, for developing the economic potential of the Highlands, offered the Campbell lairds opportunities of getting rich: timber contracts for the iron furnace established on Loch Fyne in 1754; a spinning school and factory set up at Inveraray (and later a woollen factory in the neighbourhood with the shareholders all Campbell lairds to a man); a whaling company at Campbeltown; and other such ventures.

The third Duke played a dual role—half traditional chief, half modern landlord and entrepreneur. An estate management based on dispassionate economics was still impossible. Competition for land operated within the limits set up by political security and family alliances. Economic enterprises were much in the air, but benefited mainly the Campbell lairds and gentlemen-farmers and their friends.

XXXIII

N. Nicolson, *Lord of the Isles*, London, 1960. pp. 238–42.

Judged in purely business terms, and leaving Mac Fisheries aside, the venture was therefore a complete failure. It was the only one of Leverhulme's major enterprises that was dropped at his death, or which failed to show an eventual profit. Its immediate, almost contemptuous, abandonment by Leverhulme's heirs and successors underlined the misgivings that had been constantly expressed during his lifetime, occasionally to his face by men like D'Arcy Cooper and Neil Mackay, and unreservedly behind his back. The desertion of Leverburgh made his failure in Harris even more poignant than his failure in Lewis. To those who assert that the schemes cannot truly be said to have failed because they were never carried to their logical conclusion, it should be pointed out that one of Leverhulme's main objects was that his plans should survive his death. He had given himself ten more years to live in 1918: in fact, he had seven. But during those seven years he had failed to convince even those who admired and revered him most that the foundations which he had laid were sound, or to build into his schemes the essential conditions for their continuance. They depended almost entirely upon the faith, energy and money of a single man who was already old when he embarked upon them. With his death, these three props were simultaneously snatched away, and the edifice collapsed.

Half realising this possibility, Leverhulme had pressed ahead with an urgency that was itself partly the cause of his failure. His haste antagonised the islanders more than his proposals. Any stranger to the Hebrides who has ever attempted to get a job done in a hurry, even in Stornoway, will have noticed that urgency is regarded as something improper, undignified, ungentlemanly and usually unnecessary. Long preparation and contemplation (a favourite word of the Highlander) are essential preliminaries to action. Hence the go-slow methods of the labourers in Lewis, the cynicism expressed at Leverburgh, the refusal of the women of the Bays district to have their wool spun by machine at Geocrab. They believed that change was sometimes a necessary evil, and one which could work out in the long run to their advantage; but change involved the risk of nemesis, for it meant interfering with the natural order of things, and only gradual evolution could minimise this risk. Leverhulme thought that the islands could be startled into compliance, as if by an electric shock. Ex-Provost Roderick Smith told the Town Council at his death:

It is possible that there might have been a different end to the story of Lord Leverhulme's work in Lewis, had his first early impressions of thirty years before been supplemented and nourished by one or two visits in those years in between. Such would have given his active mind a clear view of the character and forces he was subsequently to meet on these shores when he came to live among the people.

This was a subtler and a truer valediction than the usually accepted explanation of his failure, that the people did not wish to be 'civilised' by the methods that Leverhulme proposed. *The Times* obituary notice summed up the incident as follows:

Perhaps it was the one failure of Lord Leverhulme's career. He attempted to play the part of an earthly providence in the island of Lewis. The crofter population welcomed him at first when he came to establish a fishing company and promised great developments which would enormously improve their lot. But when they realised that they would have to pay for their prosperity by being, as it seemed to them, industrialised, they rebelled, and ultimately, after five years struggle, Lord Leverhulme had to accept defeat.

As this narrative has attempted to make clear, there was no 'rebellion' among the people, apart from the handful of raiders who were ostracised by all but their relations and closest neighbours. If there had been rebellion, there would have been a sense of elation in Lewis when Leverhulme withdrew. But his withdrawal was greeted not as a triumph, but with bitter disappointment and reproach. They felt let down. Never have I heard any

Lewisman say, 'Lord Leverhulme thought that he could do what he wanted with us, but we showed him that he could not. We fought him, and we won.' Such a sentiment would be quite alien to their recollection of the feeling at the time. There was rather a sense that both sides had lost a great opportunity: Leverhulme had lost it by so forcing the pace that the weaker spirits became nervous, and by failing to judge the land-question in its proper proportions; they had lost it by failing to remove the one obstacle (apart from his temporary business difficulties) that stood between him and success. Many Lewismen admit today that strong and even violent action against the raiders at the critical moment would have deprived Leverhulme of any excuse to abandon his plans. They use this harsh word 'excuse'; they believe that Leverhulme had become alarmed by the obligations in which his early impetuous enthusiasm had involved him. But this was a passing hesitancy. The excuse should not have been provided. They lacked the leader who might have shown them how to remove it.

The general charge against Leverhulme that Lewis and Harris 'refused to be industrialised' is mistaken. Attached though they were to their crofts, there were very many islanders who were willing to give Leverhulme's ideas a trial, for they accepted his argument that the only alternative was the odious policy of emigration. There was nothing in the temperament of the younger men and women that made it unthinkable for them to work in large groups for a wage, whether as members of a great fishing fleet, employees in an island factory, or sub-contractors for the tweed-mills at Stornoway. Thousands of Lewis girls were accustomed to migrate annually to work in the east-coast curing-yards, and hundreds saw no indignity in accepting posts as domestic servants in mainland cities. Certainly Lewismen might not have made such reliable workers as the mill-hands of Lancashire or the thousands who streamed daily into the vast soaperies of Port Sunlight. Absenteeism and indolence would have been frequent. But there was only a rare refusal of gang-work when it was offered to them on road and harbour construction in Lewis and Harris, or on the erection of Leverhulme's many buildings in both islands. Now that the tweed-industry has revived, and the Stornoway spinning-mills have expanded in size and number, no protest has been heard that such employment is an affront to island pride. On the contrary, thirty years after Leverhulme's death, 350 men and over 200 women were employed as factory-hands in the local mills and dye-works, and 850 men and 250 women were commuting daily into Stornoway from neighbouring townships to work in the town's factories, shops and other commercial establishments.

When one reads of the abhorrence with which the Lewismen heard the sound of a factory hooter or thought of exchanging their independence for regular employment, it is usually in a book or newspaper article by a mainlander who considers that these sentiments were the proper ones for the islanders to hold. It should be recalled that in 1920 Stornoway was not the back-water that many outsiders imagined. In its fish trade, and to a smaller extent in its tweed, it had industries which were flourishing before Leverhulme's arrival, and had already attracted to the town all the apparatus of commerce—banks, merchandising and exporting companies, a local newspaper, postal traffic, gas-lighting, a Masonic Lodge, several hotels, and a secondary school (the Nicolson Institute) that had few rivals in Scotland. Lever-hulme wished only to develop scientifically what he found. The remoter country districts, like those of any area of Great Britain which contains great industries, could have remained almost unaffected by them. Only those who chose to work for him would have felt immediately the impact of his schemes, and the possibility that the old and the new way of life would co-exist was more apparent to the Lewismen than it was to Leverhulme himself. In Harris he at last conceded by implication what he had always denied in Lewis, that the crofting system was not incompatible with limited industrialisation.

Leverhulme did not regard himself as defeated or betrayed by the islanders. Once in 1924 his secretary drafted for his signature a reply to a Uig crofter who had suggested that Uig should be joined to Harris so that this outlying district of Lewis could continue to enjoy the benefit of his schemes. The draft, in turning down the suggestion, added the phrase, 'nevertheless I appreciate the loyal spirit of the men of Uig who wish me to do so'. Leverhulme annotated: 'Never use the word "loyal" in such con-nection. Say "good".' He was anxious to avoid making it into a personal issue, being convinced that Lewis would have remained almost unanimously behind him had it not been for the attitude of the government.

The exact degree of blame that should be attached to Robert Munro remained confused in his mind. He persuaded himself that Munro was attempting to impede him by refusing to give a categorical assurance about releasing the raiders, when constitutionally Munro could not give it, and the point was not one of major importance. Leverhulme's misfortune and moral weakness was that at the very moment when Munro yielded to his demands, he was unable to take advantage of it, and looked around for other means of putting the Government in the wrong. The whole affair became a dialectical tussle between Leverhulme, Munro and, in its final phase, Lord Novar, in which the islanders themselves ceased to play much part. If the Scottish Office were wrong to assume that land-settlement was of more importance than the development of native industries, Leverhulme was wrong to choose as his battleground with the Government the one political issue on which they felt least able to give way. All his life Leverhulme had fought Governments, and as he grew older, richer and more stubborn, the possibilities of compromise appealed to him less and less. The final result, he could claim, was exactly what he forecast. The Government policy gave crofts to a few score people, who had to find subsidiary sources of income to maintain life, leaving the others no better off, and drove several thousands of young men to seek their fortune overseas. Leverhulme subtly pressed the point home by his offer to give the island to its people, and determined that in Harris he would prove the Government doubly wrong, to have enforced their own policy, and to have impeded his. From first to last he saw himself as an enlightened benefactor at war with official conservatism. He failed to see that his method of conducting the controversy would expose him to the charge of sour grapes.

Leverhulme's name is today associated by Lewismen with failure. When one suggests that it was a 'glorious' failure, the phrase does not gain assent. Lady Lever Park is still so called, and 'Leverburgh' is still printed on Ordnance maps, but no memorial was put up in his honour, not even a plaque in the church he patronised, and only recently has a road been named after him in a new housing estate at Stornoway. Elsewhere his work is known only by its ruins. The port of Leverburgh is a waste of concrete foundations; at Geocrab his machinery lies rusting in a corner; the Tolsta road has deteriorated to a cart-track; the remaining bay of the canning-factory is used for spinning wool; even the indestructible Arnish road ends forlornly in a cul-de-sac. How could £1,400,000 have been spent to so little effect? This is the question that robs Leverhulme's venture of much of its dignity, and in retrospect casts doubt on his judgment.